DWELLERS IN THE LAND

DWELLERS IN THE LAND

The Bioregional Vision

Kirkpatrick Sale

With a New Preface

The University of Georgia Press
Athens & London

Published in 2000 by the University of Georgia Press
Athens, Georgia 30602
© 1991 by Kirkpatrick Sale
Preface to the 2000 edition © 2000 by Kirkpatrick Sale
All rights reserved
Printed and bound by McNaughton & Gunn

The paper in this book meets the guidelines for
permanence and durability of the Committee on
Production Guidelines for Book Longevity of the
Council on Library Resources.

Printed in the United States of America

04   03   02   01   00   P   5   4   3   2   1

Library of Congress Cataloging-in-Publication Data

Sale, Kirkpatrick.
Dwellers in the land : the bioregional vision / Kirkpatrick Sale.
        p.   cm.
Originally published: San Francisco : Sierra Club Books, c1985.
Includes bibliographical references.
ISBN 0-8203-2205-9 (pbk. : alk. paper)
1. Ecology—Philosophy. 2. Human ecology.
3. Science—Social aspects. 4. Technology and civilization.
I. Title.
QH540.5 .S25   2000
304.2'01—DC21
99-055673

British Library Cataloging-in-Publication Data available

*This book is dedicated
to the generation on whose
shoulders I am privileged
to stand, especially my parents,
Helen Stearns and William Sale,
and E. F. Schumacher.*

Contents

Preface to the 2000 Edition

ONLY A FEW MONTHS after I finished writing this book
I decided to embark on a biography of Christopher
Columbus to be published in time for the expected
quincentennial celebration in 1992, the subtle point of which
was to contrast the sad, dispirited, violent, and nature-
hating culture of fifteenth-century Europe from which he
came with the stable, harmonious, peaceful, and nature-
loving cultures of the Americas he found. In the course of
what became too many years of research I learned a great
deal about the famous explorer, much of which had not been
covered in the numerous volumes about him, but perhaps
the most striking and most overlooked characteristic was his
tragic rootlessness, his failure ever to have a home either
before or after his voyages, his roiling drive always to go
somewhere else, sail to the next island, find the next world.
I also learned that the Spanish had then (and have now) a
word, *querencia*, that implies not merely a "love of home,"
as the dictionaries say, but, as I was to write, "a deep, quiet
sense of inner well-being that comes from knowing a particular place of the earth, its diurnal and seasonal patterns,

its fruits and scents, its history and its part in your history
... where, whenever you return to it, your soul releases an
inner sigh of recognition and relaxation." Columbus, alas,
was a man never to know *querencia*, never truly to rest in
any one place, always to go through life without that most
basic of touchstones, a home.

Querencia: very close to the bioregional vision in a word.

It was no accident, of course, that rootlessness turned out
to be a salient characteristic of the man who began the conquest of the lands that he himself more than once thought
of as paradise, for rootlessness was an abiding feature of that
restless culture from which he sprang. It still is today wherever that culture has penetrated in the world, most typically
here in the United States, which from its very beginnings
has been a mobile, questing, unsettled society and is today
so fluid that 20 percent of its population moves to a new
home every five years.

But that is just what makes bioregionalism, with a politics of place and an identification with the earth, so important as an idea and so potent as a possibility. For it speaks to
that deeply felt compulsion that no amount of wealth or
power in this fast-moving country seems ever to erase:
querencia, the need to identify with a place, to understand
one particular spot as home. This, I would argue, following
the premise of the late Rene Dubos, is an attitude that has
been part of the human experience for so long, for hundreds
of thousands of years, that it is embedded in our very
genetic makeup, and the longing continues to persist in our
souls even when our experience denies it.

Bioregionalism, of course, is only one way to talk about this
attitude, this need, and I will grant that even now, a quarter-century after the word and its ideas began to have some

currency on this continent, it is not a concept that most of mainstream America yet understands. But it has proven itself to be a singularly attractive way for a great many people to think and talk about the environments they live in and the problems and possibilities inherent there, and it has found its way into the common currency of many millions of people who are trying to identify with some particular stretch of geography as their own. That is why I think it is appropriate—and I hope useful—to have this book reissued again for the new century.

As early as 1985 the quarterly *Professional Geographer* drew the attention of the academic world to this new idea and allowed that it was a useful concept for teachers as well as activists. Subsequently several publications aimed at philosophers, including *Environmental Ethics* and *The Trumpeter,* have addressed bioregionalism in some detail, trying to identify and define the terms and theories, suggesting different ways of delineating bioregions, different ways of typing societies that live within them, and asking pertinent questions, as philosophers do, about meanings.

Then the idea began to surface in the work of landscape architects and design specialists, as a means of talking about areas in the real world that were not usefully defined by political boundaries and of seeing patterns of geography in terms of flora and fauna appropriate to them; the keynote speaker at the American Society of Landscape Architects convention in 1997 advised his audience to operate with a "bioregional hypothesis" that saw how people identified with and felt themselves as "participating members" in eco-logically defined regions. Similarly, the bioregional concept has also been used a good deal by regional planners—not surprisingly, since their profession originally was founded on watershed and other geographic givens before being seduced into "metropolitan area" gimcracks. When the Province of Ontario, for example, undertook a study in the early 1990s to reconcile the various zoning laws and planning ordinances in its jurisdiction, it explicitly recognized the Toronto area as a peninsular bioregion, much as the local Oak Ridges Bioregional group had been doing for years; a Toronto mayor has written two books on the Toronto region from a bioregional perspective. And when the state of California organized a comprehensive re-examination of environmental policies there a few years ago, bringing in the Forest Service and Bureau of Land Management, it divided the state into eleven distinct bioregions according to watersheds and specific flora and fauna and charted plans for preserving biodiversity on bioregional grounds; it even established Bioregional Councils of local residents and watershed organizations to develop and monitor policies on land use and natural resources. The federal Interior Department, too, has gotten into the act, creating Resource Advisory Councils in several western states to study land use in what are in effect bioregions, and in a few places—the Columbia River Basin, for one—it has established Ecosystem Projects.

And just last month an interesting package came to me from the U.S. Forest Service's Ecosystem Management division in Fort Collins, Colorado, with a stunning map of the "Ecoregions of North America," prepared by Robert G. Bailey. In two small insets it pictures the "Ecoregion Domains" of North America—polar, temperate, dry, and tropical—and the "Ecoregion Divisions" of the continent, a finer classification of fifteen different areas, while the main map is a careful delineation of "Ecoregion Provinces," based largely on the ecoclimate conditions and prevailing plant formations. The sixty-three provinces shown are somewhat larger than watersheds for the most part—Bailey notes that he has excluded certain measures like soil types and human settlement patterns (as well as geological, riverine, piscene, faunal, and historical indices) and so does not scale his map down to the areas I called in this book "georegions" and "morphoregions"—but the principles at work are obviously bioregional, with the provinces conforming basically to what I labeled here "ecoregions." Even more important, perhaps, the map reflects an entirely new way of thinking for the Forest Service and federal environmental planners in general that is basically bioregional, portraying the earth in terms of ecosystems instead of this resource or that, measuring nature's patterns as a whole and ignoring political and bureaucratic boundaries.

At the same time that the bioregional message has spread to organizations and professions outside the bioregional movement per se, it has also fostered a host of new groups and projects and networks within it. When Planet Drum, the California foundation that has been at the forefront of bioregional organizing from the beginning (Box 31251, San Francisco, CA 94131), put out its Directory of Bioregional Organizations in 1995, there were over 200 groups listed, up from sixty when this book was written, and there are more being added all the time. As I indicated in the chapter "Future Visions," the bioregional project has so much to recommend it as an organizing vehicle that people in all parts of the continent, seeking ways to understand their environment and the ecological methods of living within it, have taken to learning and adopting its concepts and terminologies.

A brief map-like overview of some of the most success-

ful and enduring bioregional projects suggests the scope of
the movement at the end of the century. There are self-
proclaimed bioregional groups throughout Cascadia in the
northwest (Ish Rivers and Columbiana among them), in the
Shasta bioregion of northern California, throughout Mexico
as far as Chiapas, in the Sonoran desert, in the Upper
Blackland Prairie of Texas, in the Driftless bioregion of
Wisconsin, all along the Great Lakes, in Ozarkia across the
Missouri-Arkansas border, in the Ohio Valley all the way
to Pittsburgh, in central and southern Appalachia, in the
Raritan watershed, in the Hudson Valley, in the Berkshires,
and in coastal Maine. The Ozark Area Community Congress
has had annual meetings for twenty years now, the Kansas
Area Watershed for eighteen; annual congresses recur in the
Shasta, Great Lakes, Ohio Valley, and Cascadia bioregions.
The Mattole Restoration Council in California is a coalition
of a hundred community groups and individuals that has
worked for nearly thirty years to restore salmon to the
rivers and protect the watershed's natural systems with great
if not total success; the Water Center in Eureka Springs,
Arkansas, has monitored water quality throughout the
nation for two decades and recently published a collection
of essays on water ecology; the Green City Project in San
Francisco is a network of 200 community groups that work
to turn the city greener by seeing it within a bioregional
context rather than as an urban isolate; the E. F. Schumacher
Society in the Berkshires has spent twenty years promot-
ing the principles of local currencies and community
economics as a means of regional empowerment, and its
library is an important center of bioregional information;
an Institute for Bioregional Studies on Prince Edward
Island has run programs on a wide range of environmental

and community development issues for many years. And all of these have been theoretically drawn together in an umbrella organization, the Bioregional Association of the Northern Americas (BANA), that was formed in 1996 to try to give a unified voice to the movement and provide resources and information for both new and developed bioregional groups; BANA is currently being coordinated by the heroic people at Planet Drum.

Another important measure of the continued impact of bioregionalism is the publication of a little bioregional library by two Canadians, Judith and Christopher Plant, operating first as the *New Catalyst* magazine and then as New Society Publishers (Box 189, Gabriola Island, British Columbia, VOR 1X0). So far they have brought out *Turtle Talk: Voices for a Sustainable Future; Green Business: Hope or Hoax?; Putting Power in Its Place: Create Community Control!; Living with the Land: Communities Restoring the Earth; Circles of Strength: Community Alternatives to Alienation;* and *Boundaries of Home: Mapping for Local Empowerment.* More volumes are promised, but it is already an important educational achievement few movements can boast of. And the wider bioregional library also includes all the myriad books that have been produced by bioregional authors in the years since this book was first published; too numerous to list in full—there are certainly several hundred that incorporate a bioregional perspective—they include such works as Thomas Berry's *The Dream of the Earth,* J. M. Jamie Brownson's *In Cold Margins: Sustainable Development in Northern Bioregions,* Chellis Glendinning's *Off the Map,* Freeman House's *Totem Salmon,* Jerry Mander's *In the Absence of the Sacred,* Kenton Miller's *Balancing the Scales: Guidelines for*

Increasing Biodiversity's Chances through Bioregional Management, Stephanie Mills's *In Service of the Wild: Restoring and Reinhabiting Damaged Land*, and Charlene Spretnak's *Resurgence of the Real*.

Mention, too, should be made of the international dimension of bioregionalism, much developed in recent years. Probably the most important extension has been southward into Mexico and Central America to include the rest of the continent that has become the geographic symbol of the movement, named Turtle Island after an Indian creation myth (of which more later). Because of the efforts of several groups in Mexico City, Morelos, Maruata, and elsewhere, two of the biannual movement get-togethers (originally called North American Bioregional Congresses, which drew up movement platforms, now changed to Turtle Island Bioregional Gatherings, more for socializing) were held in Mexico, and a south-of-the-border presence is now fixed in most continental activities and deliberations. Substantial bioregional meetings have also been held in Medellín, Colombia, and Bahia de Craquez, Ecuador, in recent years. Europe has always been hospitable to the bioregional vision, now an explicit part of Green party organizing on the subcontinent ("A Europe of the Regions" is one of the Green slogans); small bioregional groups operate in England, France, Italy, and Spain, and a Bioregional Document Center has recently been established in Italy. Japan has similarly always been fertile ground for bioregional ideas, and a group of environmentalists protesting the 1998 Olympics at Nagano for its damage to the Himegawa watershed (with the slogan "Nobody Wins the Games If Nature Loses") used bioregional terms and concepts in its campaign.

In one area where the bioregional apparatus should have been zealously seized upon, however, the results have been disappointing. This is in Indian country in North America, among the tribes and reservations that have within them a substantial number of people, from young turks to revered elders, who are trying to keep tribal traditions and perceptions alive, even making them useful tools for contemporary struggles—a natural bioregional seedbed. A few distinguished leaders—among them Oren Lyons, Faithkeeper of the Onondagas, and John Mohawk, a professor of American Studies at SUNY Buffalo—have indeed embraced bioregionalism, which is after all nothing more than a modern version of ancient tribal understandings that shaped and guided Indian societies for centuries. But a misguided sense that the movement is Anglocentric has impeded the message reaching into as many Indian communities as it might logically find, despite real efforts by bioregionalists in general to make contacts, and more work will need to be done before the alliance is fully forged.

I mentioned at the beginning of this preface that bioregionalism is only one of many ways to address the issue of *querencia* and its denials in modern culture. Happily, many of the other responses have grown with as much energy as the bioregional movement in the last two decades, mixing and interconnecting in a way that has established what might be called an *ecocentric* perspective as an ineradicable part of contemporary social thought. They each have run their individual courses, to be sure, but they all also feed into the bioregional stream, strengthening and enlarging it.

Perhaps the most important of these synergistic compan-

ions is deep ecology, the "ecosophy" that Arne Naess and
George Sessions and others created in the 1980s (though
the term was coined as early as 1973) as a contrast to the
shallow ecology practiced by most mainstream environmental groups. It is complex, but in essence it stresses the equality of all species and the obligation of the human to fit within
the web of being so as to allow other life-forms to flourish
as much as possible; it is life-centered, in other words, rather
than human-centered. The idea had been a sort of unspo-
ken underpinning of bioregionalism, but the deep ecology
philosophers have given it explicit and eloquent expression
in several books (e.g., George Sessions's anthology, *Deep
Ecology for the Twenty-first Century*), countless articles, and
one thirteen-part radio series (including one tape on "The
Bioregional Perspective") distributed nationally by New
Dimensions Radio; there is also a well-funded Foundation
for Deep Ecology, established to advance its themes and
causes.

Other allied responses of the last two decades, somewhat
less philosophical, include the widespread adoption of local
currencies and exchanges (in at least 1,000 communities
worldwide) and development of groups for regional economic self-sufficiency; the strong crusade for organic food
and organic agriculture, along with local greenmarkets,
inevitably region-based; community-supported agriculture,
which has been spread to some 800 communities in the
U.S. within a decade; "eco-villages" and other designed
communities that are consciously set into their environments in ways that minimize human impact and maximize
biodiversity; alternative medicine, particularly the herbal
and local-vegetation side of it; organizing against the
global economy and its free-trade pacts that stifle and

smother local enterprises and initiatives, an effort spear-headed now by a coalition called the International Forum on Globalization, founded in 1995, and people connected to *The Ecologist* magazine.

Less successful than these in winning adherents and developing bioregional thinking has been the Green politics movement in the U.S. Though Green parties continue to be reasonably successful in Europe (and the German Greens are part of the governing coalition), the various Green manifestations here have had little success beyond the elections of a municipal judge here and a city councilor there. That the movement has not lived up to the promise I anticipated for it fifteen years ago probably has to do with the deficiency I feared from the start: its refusal to make ecological analysis—and bioregional thinking—the centerpiece of its politics and its misguided attempt instead to make that only one element of a scattershot ten-point platform. As a result it has confined itself to a tiny liberal niche in the conventional electoral system instead of identifying and energizing alternative units, at community and bioregional levels, that might promise real political change.

As I explained in my original preface to this book, I was led to bioregionalism when I first learned about it in the 1970s because to my reading it expressed in a deep and comprehensive form the essential ideals that I think are crucial for a viable human society on this singular planet: ecological understanding, regional and communitarian consciousness, nature-based wisdom and spirituality, biocentric sensibility, decentralist planning, participatory politics, mutual aid, and speciate humility. I have not since come across any other philosophy or worldview that improves on that, and the growing environmental crisis, in many ways worse than it was fifteen years ago, now only convinces me more than ever that it is "a crucial, and perhaps virtually the only possible, means of arresting the impending ecological apocalypse"— if it can be halted at all.

As I said then, "I hope you will understand and come to share that perception, feel that urgency, and ultimately become energized by that vision. Because what other choice, really, do we have?"

In one form of an old Indian legend it is said that, in the beginning, the Great Originator made two worlds before this world: but on the first, the creatures were bad and did not know how to live, so it was destroyed with fire, and on the second the creatures were stupid and did not know how to live, so it was destroyed with water. When the whole universe was under water, the Great Originator decided to try one more time, and told the creatures to swim to the bottom of the water and find some mud with which to make the earth of a new world.

The loon swooped down with its graceful dive, but it brought back nothing: "The water is too deep," it said. "I could not reach the bottom." Then the otter dove in with its powerful webbed feet, but it brought back nothing: "The water is too deep," it said. "I could not reach the bottom." Next went the beaver with its great propelling tail, but even it was unable to bring back the mud: "The water is too deep. I could not reach the bottom."

Finally, the turtle, who was very strong and very patient and able to live for a very long time, swam down in the water, and stayed down for such a long time the other animals feared it had drowned. Then, after a very, very long time— it may have been centuries—the turtle reappeared out of the water, with a great mass of mud covering its shell, and cried to the Great Originator: "I found the bottom, and here is your mud. Now make us a new world!"

The Great Originator took the mud and began to spread it, shaping it into great plains and mountains and deserts, until it covered all the water but a few lakes and rivers and streams. Next the Great Originator clapped its hands and there were other creatures on the land, birds and insects and fish and plants and trees, and then with another clap appeared men and women and children, red and white and black and yellow, and they too were spread over the land.

Then the Great Originator spoke: "On the first world the creatures were bad and on the second world the creatures were stupid, so I destroyed both of them. Now I have given all of you a third world, and if you learn to live upon it with reverence and harmony, living in peace with each other, the two-legged and the four-legged and the many-legged, the swimmers and the fliers and the crawlers, the plants and flowers and trees, the waters and the soils, then all will be well. But if you are bad or stupid, and make this world ugly, and sick, and unhappy, then I will destroy this world, too. It is up to you."

And the Great Originator named this world Turtle Island, in honor of the creature who had found the mud from which it was made, and then he placed the earth on top of the turtle so it would forever be a reminder to all other creatures of the animal that carries its home on its back throughout its life, and must protect and preserve its home because its home protects and preserves it.

That is a message taken to heart by many of the societies originally inhabiting this land, why they thought of their world as Turtle Island, and why they developed cultures that would heed the Great Originator's warning. That is a message taken to heart, these many centuries later, by the movement that has taken the turtle as its totem animal and ultimately would seek to emulate those societies and their stable, harmonious, peaceful, and nature-loving ways: their *querencia.*

Besides, the turtle is an animal that gets ahead only by sticking its neck out. And it eventually wins the race.

Preface to the 1991 Edition

SINCE IT MAY be fairly said that "bioregion" is not exactly a household word in America and the idea of a "bioregional vision" not yet likely to resonate in many American bosoms, it seems clear that an introductory effort is in order—and that is precisely the role this book seeks to fulfill.

It is obviously not an everything-you-ever-wanted-to-know-about book, since the field of bioregionalism, new though it is, has already amassed a huge body of information, experience, analysis, and wisdom that would fill many volumes several times the size of this one. It is obviously also not a final-word-set-in-stone book, because the bioregional effort is still in its youth and is uncovering new insights, territories, and linkages all the time. And it is not a definitive-down-from-the-Mount book either, for bioregionalism is fluid and organic, with perhaps as many approaches as there are bioregionalists, among which mine is only one.

This book is rather an attempt, early on in the bioregional project, to lay some of its groundwork, suggest some of its basic outlines, and gather in one place some of its wisdom, so that we will be able to encourage thought, and discussion, and some basic hard work, within the movement and without. It is my own vision I put forth here, and though I have read widely in this and related areas, though I have talked with many hundreds of people who identify themselves as bioregionalists, and though I think I fairly present the mainstream principles of bioregionalism, this book cannot—and does not—pretend to speak for all bioregionalists. Who, Lord knows, have given ample evidence that they can speak for themselves.

· · ·

I have been led to this consideration of the shape of the bioregional vision, inevitably as it were, by the trajectory of my previous work: on American radicalism, on American regionalism, on the abject failure of American giantism. It expresses for me not merely the newest and most comprehensive form of the ideals of decentralism, participation, liberation, mutualism, and community that I have expounded in all that work—but, as it stems from the most elemental perception of the crises of the planet, the ideals of ecological sanity, regional consciousness, speciate humility, and global survival. It is for me, therefore, not merely a new way of envisioning and enacting a very old American ideal, but also a crucial, and perhaps virtually the only possible, means of arresting the impending ecological apocalypse.

I hope you will understand and come to share that perception, feel that urgency, and ultimately become energized by that vision. Because what other choice, really, do we have?

Acknowledgments

MY DEEP AND sincere thanks to Peter Berg, Gary Coates, Carlotta Collette, David Ehrenfeld, Pliny Fisk, Maurice Girodias, Teddy Goldsmith, David Gurin, David Haenke, Michael Helm, Ron Hughes, Kelly Kindscher, Fred Kreuger, Tanya Kucak, Sibyl Levue, Perry Mackey, Michael Marien, Paul McIsaac, John McClaughry, Victor Navasky, Helena Norberg-Hodge, John Papworth, Ray Reece, Norman Rush, Paul Ryan, Roger Sale, Jaap Spek, Charlene Spretnak, Bob Swann, George Tukel, Gail Vittori, Susan Witt, and Rob Young; my special thanks to the E. F. Schumacher Society, to all those who have so thoughtfully responded to my WBAI radio program, "Human Scale," and to all past and present bioregionalists.

I am in special debt to my editor Danny Moses, and, as always, to my family, Rebekah, Kalista, and my dear and special wife, Faith.

I

The Bioregional Heritage

The greatest beauty is
Organic wholeness, the wholeness of life and things, the
divine beauty of the universe. Love that, not man
Apart from that.

Robinson Jeffers, "The Answer"

Technology, masquerading as an end rather than a means,
has unnecessarily moved man away from nature, and in so
doing has moved him away from himself.

David Ehrenfeld, *Conserving Life on Earth*

ONE

Gaea

IN THE BEGINNING, as the Greeks saw it, when chaos settled into form there was a mighty sphere, floating free within the moist, gleaming embrace of the sky and its great swirling drifts of white cloud, a vibrant globe of green and blue and brown and gray, binding together in a holy, deep-breasted synchrony the temperatures of the sun, the gasses of the air, the chemicals of the sea, the minerals of the soil, and bearing the organized, self-contained, and almost purposeful aspect of a single organism, *alive*, a breathing, pulsing body that was, in the awed words of Plato, "a living creature, one and visible, containing within itself all living creatures."

To this the Greeks gave a name: Gaea, the earth mother. She was the mother of the heavens, Uranus, and of time, Cronus; of the Titans and the Cyclops; of the Meliae, the ash-tree spirits who were the progenitors of all humankind; the mother of all, first of the cosmos, creator of the creators. She became the symbol of all that was sacred and the source of all that was wise, and at the fissures and rifts in her surface—at Delphi, especially, and at Olympia and Dodona—she would impart her knowledge to those few mortals, the oracles, who knew how to hear it.

"Earth is a goddess," wrote Xenophon in the 4th century before Christ, "and teaches justice to those who can learn." Justice, yes, and the other attributes later called—interestingly—the *natural* virtues: prudence, a knowledge of natural limits; fortitude, an appreciation of natural realities; and temperance, an awareness of natural restraints. "The better she is served," Xenophon went on to teach, "the more good things she gives in return," a classical wisdom the Homeric-era "Hymn to Earth" renders thus:

> To Gaea, mother of all of life and oldest of gods, I sing,
> You who make and feed and guide all creatures of the earth,
> Those who move on your firm and radiant land, those who
> > wing
> Your skies, those who swim your seas, to all these you have
> > given birth;
> Mistress, from you come all our harvests, our children, our
> > night and day,
> Yours the power to give us life, yours to take away.
> > To you, who contain everything,
> > To Gaea, mother of all, I sing.

Inevitably Gaea became embodied in the language of the Greeks as the word for the earth itself, and it is from her that we derive such English words as *geography* (in Greek *gaia* or *ge*, earth—plus *graphien*, to write or describe), *geometry*, *geomancy*, *geology*, and the like. For the Greeks, Gaea also came to symbolize life itself, and birth and origination, so her name was combined into the word *genos*—life—from which we take such English words as *genesis*, *genus*, *genitals*, *genetics*, and *generation*. (The realization of this may help to promote the spelling of the name as *Gaea* and pronunciation as *jee-ah*, as it is rendered in most English dictionaries. Although in Greek orthography the name was rendered as the equivalent of *Gaia*, pronounced *guy-ah*, the only

4

explanation of why the British insist on that form instead of the mellifluous one in their own language is that they are employing the same facility for sound that leads them to use "Venice" for Venezia and "Florence" for Firenze.)

. . .

The wisdom of the Greeks was not theirs alone. In fact, among the earliest societies it appears with such regularity across every continent, no matter what the climate or geography, and in every preliterate culture, that we may fairly think of it as a basic, almost innate, human perception. In virtually every hunter-gatherer society that archeologists have discovered from the paleolithic past, in almost every rudimentary society that anthropologists have studied in recent centuries, one of the central deities—in many cases the primary god, worshipped before all others—was the earth.

There is no special mystery to it. In societies whose very existence depended upon knowing the earth and how to hunt its animals and forage for its foods—the way of life for 99 percent of human history—respect for the natural world and an appreciation of the land itself as sacred and inviolable was surely inevitable. That sensibility was literally so vital that it was embedded in some central place in each culture's myths and traditions and was embodied in each culture's supreme spirits and deities.

For these early human peoples, the world around and all its features—rivers, trees, clouds, springs, mountains—were regarded as alive, endowed with spirit and sensibility every bit as real as those of humans, and in fact of exactly the same type and quality as a human's: among the Iroquois this was called *orenda*, the invisible force inherent in all parts of the universe, and in certain Bantu languages the same presence is known as *mata*.

5

Animals had souls, of course, so in all hunting societies some form of ritual apology and forgiveness was necessary before the kill: hence the Navajo praying to the deer before the hunt, the Mbuti cleansing themselves by smoke each morning, the Naskapi pledging to the hunted, "You and I have the same mind and spirit." But plants and flowers and trees had spirits, too, every bit as sensate, so almost all early peoples had elaborate ceremonies connected with cutting and harvesting, asking exoneration for the painful removal of some of Mother Earth's children, and most had stories like the Ojibways', which speak of "the wailing of the trees under the axe," or like the ancient Chinese tales which mention cries of "pain and indignation" from fallen branches. Hence the well-nigh universal phenomenon that anthropologists, until recently, liked to dismiss as "tree-worshipping": treating certain local trees, or groves, or whole forests as especially sacred and sacrosanct, in innate recognition of the fundamental, life-sustaining function of arboreal life on earth. From the Celts in the West to the Yalta tribes in the East, and from the Finns in the North to the Greeks in the South, trees and forests occupied a special place of spiritual honor throughout ancient Europe. Indeed among northern German tribes the Teutonic word for *temple* actually meant forest, and in Greek the word *neos*, a holy sanctuary, implied not a human-built but a natural enclosure.*

Among such nature-based peoples there was no separation of the self from the world such as we have come to learn, no division between the human (willed, thinking, superior) and the non-human (conditioned, insensate, inferior). Much of

---

* The power of such "tree-worshipping" has not entirely vanished: hence the Yule log, Christmas trees, mistletoe, harvest bowers, wedding bouquets, flowers associated with Christian holy days, and even knocking wood for luck.

the world was highly mysterious, to be sure, and many phenomena were unexplainable, but there was at the same time a liberating, psychically healthy sense of wholeness, of oneness, of place. As anthropologist Jack Forbes has said about the early California Indian tribes:

> They perceived themselves as being deeply bound together with other people (and with the surrounding non-human forms of life) in a complex interconnected web of life, that is to say, a true community. . . . All creatures and all things were . . . brothers and sisters. From this idea came the basic principle of non-exploitation, of respect and reverence for all creatures.

Indicative of this bond is that for most of these societies the identity with the earth was so strong that their legends about creation commonly told of humanity itself emerging from a hole in the ground, or a cleft in the rocks, or the depths of a tree: the Mbuti in the Congolese rainforest, for example, say the very first human emerged from the inside of a mahogany tree, the Pueblo Indians that people climbed out of the "womb of the earth."

As a matter of fact we retain this identity in our languages today, though we, alas, no longer appreciate the association: the Indo-European word for earth, *dhghem*, is the root of the Latin *humanus*, the Old German *guman*, and the Old English *guman*, all of which meant "human." The only remnant of this sensibility I can think of today in our everyday language is *humus*, the rich, organic soil in which things grow best, though we no longer make the same connections the Latins did when we use the word.

· · ·

It is natural but significant nonetheless that the deity of the earth in many societies was a woman, for the fecundity of both would be immediately obvious to any established society. This would be particularly true where, as was common until recently, the role of paternity was quite unknown and the woman's ability to give birth was as astonishing and wonderful—and necessary—as the earth's ability to regenerate itself in spring.

For the peoples of the Mediterranean and the Near East—as for the early Greeks—the Earth Goddess was at the center of spiritual constructs. Figures of "the mother goddess" are found in sacred shrines dating as far back as the Aurignacian cultures of 25,000 BC; excavations of Jarmo (6800 BC), Catal Hayuk (6500 BC), Halaf (5000 BC), Ur (4000 BC), and Elam (3000 BC) all indicate that female goddesses, and probably female priests as well, were dominant in their early religions. In Sumeria the goddess Nammu was "the mother who gave birth to heaven and earth"; in Egypt Isis was the "oldest of the old . . . from whom all becoming arose"; in Turkey the goddess Arinna was worshipped above all others, and "no other deity is as honored or great"; in Babylon Ishatar was the Queen of Heaven, "goddess of the universe [who] out of chaos brought us harmony." She was Cybele in Phrygia, Astarte in Phoenicia, Ashtoreth to the Hebrews, Athar in Syria. And her direct counterparts are found among the Irish, the Innuit Eskimos, the Japanese, the Iroquois, the Finns, the Khasis of India, the Lepcha of Sikkim, the Tallensi of West Africa.

The Roman writer Lucius Apuleius, writing in the 2d century AD, personified the Earth Goddess this way:

> I am Nature, the universal Mother, mistress of all elements, primordial child of time, sovereign of all things spiritual, queen of the dead, queen also of the immortals, the single manifestation of all gods and goddesses that are.
>
> My nod governs the shining heights of Heaven, the wholesome sea breezes, the lamentable silences of the world below.

Though I am worshipped in many aspects, known by countless names, and propitiated with all manner of different rites, yet the whole round earth venerates me.

The primeval Phrygians call me Pessinuntica, Mother of the gods; the Athenians sprung from their own soil, call me Cecropian Artemis; for the islanders of Cyprus I am Paphian Aphrodite, for the archers of Crete I am Dictynna; for the trilingual Silicians, Stygian Prosperine; and for the Eleusinians their ancient Mother of Corn.

Some know me as Juno, some as Bellona of the Battles; others as Hecate, others again as Rhamnubia, but both races of Aethiopians, whose lands the morning sun first shines upon, and the Egyptians who excel in ancient learning and worship me with ceremonies proper to my godhead, call me by my true name, namely Queen Isis.

So powerful was this Gaean tradition, so rooted in what seems to have been more than twenty millennia of religious culture, that even the male-god Indo-Europeans who invaded the Mediterranean world in about 4500 BC and successfully imposed their values on many cultures in their path could not displace it. Male deities were introduced with apparently greater frequency after this period—the Greek pantheon shifted, to take but one example, and Zeus, Adonis, and the like began appearing from about 2000 BC—but at no time were the female deities entirely supplanted, even among the ancient Hebrews. It was not until fairly late on that Judaism, then Christianity, and then Islam finally succeeded in effectively purging most forms of goddess worship from the religious cultures of the area.

Even then, however, even with the triumph of male monotheism throughout most of the Mediterranean and European worlds, even with the displacement of earth-worship for various abstract kinds of sky-worship, and even with the placement of the human (male) above all other creatures of the world—*even then* the notion of an animate earth did not completely die, certainly not among the general mass of people, religious believers or not. For all but a few, no matter what the culture or god, the world and its parts still were regarded as endowed with life and spirit and purpose, sometimes knowable to humans, or discernible, more often not. Rivers and waves and clouds and winds, obviously, were living, and trees and flowers and grasses, and fire and lightning and rain and snow—these all could be seen to move, after all—but also stones and clods of earth and mountains. In the words of historian Morris Berman:

> The view of nature which predominated in the West down to the eve of the Scientific Revolution was that of an enchanted world. Rocks, trees, rivers, and clouds were all seen as wondrous, alive, and human beings felt at home in this environment. The cosmos, in short, was a place of *belonging*. A member of this cosmos was not an alienated observer of it but a direct participant in its drama. His personal destiny was bound up with its destiny, and this relationship gave meaning to his life.

In all the long stretch of human history, it seems, from our very beginnings as tribal beings 30,000 years ago right down through classical and medieval times, until sometime in the last 400 years, the people of this planet saw themselves as inhabitants within a world alive.

. . .

When the first photographs were published of the earth as seen from the moon, the ancient Gaean perspective suddenly was given new confirmation. There was no mistaking the fact that the earth appeared in every way to be a living being, the

10

only thing in all the vast, drear reaches of space except the sun itself that had color and movement and, somehow, the look of purposeful organization, much the way certain living cells look when seen through a microscope.

Dr. Lewis Thomas, the eminent biologist and renowned author, was among those struck by these photographs. In his eye-opening little book, *The Lives of a Cell*, he wrote:

> Viewed from the distance of the moon, the astonishing thing about the earth, catching the breath, is that it is alive. The photographs show the dry, pounded surface of the moon in the foreground, dead as an old bone. Aloft, floating green beneath the moist, gleaming membrane of bright blue sky, is the rising earth, the only exuberant thing in this part of the cosmos. If you could look long enough, you would see the swirling of the great drifts of white cloud, covering and uncovering the half-hidden masses of land. If you had been looking for a very long, geologic time, you could have seen the continents themselves in motion, drifting apart on their crustal plates, held afloat by the fire beneath. It has the organized, self-contained look of a live creature.

To which, if he had gone on to christen it, he would undoubtedly have given the name "Gaea."

TWO

Gaea Abandoned

As BENEVOLENT as she is, however, Gaea is capable of revenge.

The Mycenaean civilization that flourished on the Aegean islands and coasts in the second millennium before Christ, say from 1600 to 1000 BC, inspired the Homeric stories, those legends of great cities and heroic dynasties, and even they failed to do justice to the complexity and grandeur of that early culture. As H. R. Trevor-Roper has said:

> The poet exaggerates whenever numbers come in—of slaves and heroes and gold tripods and cattle—yet his overblown figures are tiny compared with the quantities inscribed on the [Mycenaean] tablets. The lords of Mycenae . . . controlled far more extensive holdings in land and cattle and slaves . . . than the heroes who fought in Homer's Troy.

It was a sophisticated society, with written records and a developed economy—something like a hundred different agricultural and industrial occupations were listed in the Mycenaean records—and one that sustained a prosperous system of trade and a ruling stratum with elaborate buildings, extensive land and cattle holdings, and art and artifacts of considerable richness.

It seems that the Mycenaeans were not Greeks, strictly speaking, but they clearly adopted the Greek concept of the Earth Mother, Gaea, and sustained the elaborate Greek celebrations of her wisdom, creativity, sexuality, and fecundity; surviving artifacts show that Mycenaean shrines, probably the responsibility of a priestess caste, honored the generosity, the majesty, and the unpredictability of the goddess, her soil, her foods, her waters.

Yet somewhere, somehow, the poisons crept in. It might have been from *without*, from the so-called Dorians (probably the male-god Indo-Europeans) from the steppes of Europe, who, as art historian Vincent Scully puts it, suppressed "the old concept of the dominance of the goddess of the earth herself, seizing the sovereign power by virtue of their own thunder-wielding sky god, Zeus," and destroyed "the old, simple, almost vegetable unity between man and nature." Or it might have come from *within*, from the decadence and carelessness, the sheer hubris of cultures that in their latter days grow too large and distended (like the Egyptians, the Persians, the Romans, the Spanish, the Toltecs, and the modern Americans, among many), for it is then that they become more concerned with exploitation and domination than nurturance and sustainability, with the riches of ores rather than the riches of the soil, with preserving bureaucracy and hierarchy rather than ecosystems and habitats.

Whatever the reason, the ways of Gaea were forgotten. Over the years the Mycenaeans systematically cut down the holly, cypress, olive, pine, and sycamore trees that originally covered the Mediterranean slopes, using the wood for fuel and lumber—and often as much for export, and empty riches, as for themselves. The deforested hills, unreplenished, collapsed, their topsoils and minerals washed away in the torrential Mediterranean rains, and great gouges eroded into once-fertile hillsides. Herding of goats, cattle, and swine as well as sheep became a common practice, quite heedless of the multiple effects on the countryside. It wasn't bad enough that the animals' hooves destroyed groundcover and compacted the soils, and that their teeth devoured leaves and twigs in addition to grasses, but the herders even took to setting fire to the forests to open up more areas for their flocks.

The devastation was swift and thorough, indelibly fresh in Plato's mind even seven or eight centuries later: "What now remains compared with what then existed," he wrote, "is like the skeleton of a sick man, all the fat and soft earth having been wasted away, and only the bare framework of the land being left."

And thus descended the Greek Dark Ages. The Mycenaean culture collapsed, apparently within the astonishingly short period of two generations. For the next 500 years—a considerable stretch of time, equal to the one that separates us from Columbus—Greece suffered the consequences of its heedless rapaciousness. Something like *90 percent* of the population died off or emigrated north and west to more fructuous land. Those that survived and remained lived in small, scattered settlements, eking out meager lives on the exhausted soils. Great thriving cities shrank to small villages or vanished completely, leaving the Aegean coasts bare and depopulated. The literacy of the Mycenaean society vanished, to be replaced by oral folktales (out of which the Homeric epics come), and the rich artistic traditions dwindled to rude fabrication.

Not more than a hundred years after the height of a flourishing Mycenaean culture, the Aegean seas were witness to a pallid, poor, crude, and decimated population scarcely deserving of the word "civilization."

. . .

The Mycenaean Greeks were not the only ones through history who, having abandoned the worship and having forgotten the lessons of Gaea, were taught to their dismay the hard lessons of ecological hubris. Later on the Romans, whose cumulative assaults on the Mediterranean ecology were almost certainly a central factor in the collapse of their empire—and the Sumerians, the Harappans, the Mayans, the Chinese of at least the T'ang and Han dynasties, and numerous other imperial peoples who matched their dominance of humans with their dominance of nature, were forced to learn these inescapable truths.

But in no previous society did the abandonment of Gaea reach the scale it reached in Europe in the centuries after the Renaissance, the period of which we today are the exuberant consummation. For with the development of that branch of learning which usurped the word "science"—in the classical world it meant knowledge of all kinds, in the European world it was reserved for the study of a separate thing called "the natural world"—and which has dominated most intellectual and social life since the 16th century virtually all animistic, all venerative, all religious conceptions of the earth were deposed. In their stead came a new vision supported by the incontrovertible findings of physics, chemistry, mechanics, astronomy, and mathematics: the scientific worldview.

The new perception held—better than that, it *proved*—that the earth, the universe beyond it, and all within it operated according to certain clear, calculable, and unchanging laws, not by the whims of any living, sentient being. It showed that these laws were, far from being divinely created or spiritually inspired, capable of mundane scientific measurement, prediction, and replication, even scientific manipulation and control. It demonstrated that the objects of the universe, from the smallest stone to the earth's orb itself and the planets beyond, were not animate or purposeful, with individual souls and wills and spirits, but were nothing more than combinations of certain chemical and mechanical properties. It established beyond all doubt that there are not one but *two* worlds, the mechanical and inert one out there, made up of a random collection of insensate atoms, and the human one within, where thought and purpose and consciousness reside.

It achieved, in Schiller's matchless phrase, "*die Entgotterung der Natur*"—the "de-godding" of nature.

Bacon, Descartes, Newton, Galileo, all of the masterful minds of 16th- and 17th-century science, swept away, in only a few generations, the accumulated nonsense of the animistic past, much of which still lingered on even in the Europe of that time. To think of the cosmos as alive, to identify the dead matter of the earth with the organic spirit of human beings, was childish, barbarian, naive. If there was an image for the cosmos, it was not that of a goddess or any other being but something like what Newton spoke of as a giant clock, a Cosmick Machine, its many parts moving in an ordered, kinetic, mechanical way. As 17th-century physicist Robert Hooke put it, the scientific revolution enabled humankind "to discover all the secret workings of Nature, almost in the same manner as we do those that are the productions of Art and are manag'd by Wheels, and Engines, and Springs." And if God was allowed to play a part—for indeed these were all nominal Christians—he was given a role as little more than a clock-winder: "It seems probable to me," Newton wrote in 1730, "that God in the beginning formed matter in solid, massy, hard, impenetrable, movable particles, of such sizes and figures, and with such other properties and in such proportion to space as most conduced to the end for which He formed them."

Slowly and powerfully, with a growth both geometric and relentless, the ideas of the scientific paradigm transformed completely the attitudes of Western society toward nature and the cosmos. Nature was no longer either beautiful or scary but merely *there*, not to be worshipped or celebrated, but more often than not to be *used*, with all the ingenuity and instruments of a scientific culture—gingerly at times, wholeheartedly at others, within limits if need be, heedless of limits if possible, but used—*by* humans, *for* humans.

Is that too harsh? Take as an example Europe's treatment of the New World that opened up at the same time as the rise of science and the nation-states that nurtured it. Two continents, pristine jewels of unimagined glories, were perceived as nothing but empty spaces for unwanted populations, repositories of wanted ores, tracts of trees to fell and fields to plow, virgin territories with no other purpose but to be *worked*. Those who inhabited those spaces could be honorably and properly displaced, for they were only hunters and foragers who did nothing to "improve" the land and thus had no standing in the eyes of European law. Within a single century the Spanish denuded the New World of most of its gold, quite regardless of the human destruction they wrought; within a century and a half the lands available for crops desired in Europe were being recklessly ravaged, with forced labor imported at the rate of 100,000 slaves a year; within another half-century the massive deforestation known as the Midwest Clearcut eliminated 100,000 acres of trees; within two generations the populations of prairie bison were reduced almost to extinction; and of course the sorry list could go on. And the example was multiplied around the world.

The scientific revolution is often regarded as beginning with the perfection of the first compound microscope—probably by Zacharia Janssen around 1590, and that seems an especially appropriate symbol. Far from contemplating the intermeshings of the cosmos, the mystery of a heaven-full of stars, and the miracle of the seasons—the process, we may imagine, by which the early societies came to their concept of the Living Earth—the experimenters of modern science looked downward, searching for the tiniest and simplest forms through a small manipulable machine. There is something haunting in that image—especially when you realize that the scientist at the microscope is always half-blind—and in the birth of that instrument we may see the death of Gaea.

. . .

Every society selects its own myths, its own cosmologies. As the ancient Greeks chose to fabricate the persona of Gaea, so the European establishment of the 16th and 17th centuries chose to adopt the worldview of mechanistic science. But such choices are not made by accident; there is always a cause. In the history of ideas, as in the history of technologies, those developments that suit the powers-that-be are embraced, those deemed to have no utility are ignored.

Let me give an example from the realm of technology. Sometime around the birth of Christ, eighteen centuries before James Watt, Hero of Alexandria created a steam engine. It worked well enough, and it may even have been used to open the doors of a local temple, but no one thought to develop the principle and Hero's sketches for this revolutionary invention remained buried in his notebooks. The Mediterranean powers of the time, you see, had no need for such a device, because any such onerous mechanical tasks as Hero's machine could do were already being done by slaves or minions. It was not

until the 18th century, in an England where slavery was out-
lawed and the need for mechanical power was acute, that the
virtues of steam power were appreciated sufficiently to enlist
whole ranks of investors and rows of inventors—and ultimately the Watt machine was perfected. Even then, it was a
conscious decision by lawmakers of Parliament and the investors of the City that allowed this particular device to be favored
above all others and supported as the principal driving force
of the Industrial Revolution.

Similarly, the dominant elements of 17th- and 18th-cen-
tury Europe accepted the scientific worldview so quickly and
thoroughly because it so smoothly and effectively filled their
economic and political needs. It provided both the intellectual
substructure and the practical mechanisms for the rise of the
nation-state out of feudal localism, for their chosen system of
mercantile and industrial capitalism, and for their enterprise
of global colonialism and exploitation.

Of course this interrelationship was far from simple, and
the intricacies of it all may be found, for example, in the writ-
ings of Tawney, Whitehead, Wallerstein, Berman, Braudel,
and other scholarly sources. But it is easy enough to see that
certain aspects of the new science would be welcomed by the
established powers of the time: the celebration of the mechanical, the tangible, the quantifiable, the utilitarian, the linear,
and the divisible, as against the organic, the spiritual, the in-
calculable, the mysterious, the circular, and the holistic. For
the new *nationalism* that wished to establish its control over
all secular matters by immutable laws and to regard its deni-
zens as measurable and manipulable objects, and for the new
capitalism that wished to oversee the materialistic and impersonal marketplace and to develop and exploit the new-found
colonial territories, the underlying principles of the scientific
ideology were obviously ideal.

Above all, science's profoundly new way of regarding the natural world—as some lifeless abstract to be controlled and used for human ends, with humans acting, in Descartes' phrase, as "masters and possessors of Nature"—was ardently embraced as the vital centerpiece of European culture, the one setting it off from all other societies of the past, the one allowing humans at last to take their "rightful" place in the center of the terrestrial stage.

Thus it was that the scientific worldview came to have an immense and by now almost unimaginable impact on the European world, far beyond whatever experiments went on in the laboratories or whatever inventions came out of the workshops. Primed, supported, and elaborated by its powerful sponsors, science was a perception, even a philosophy, that in a remarkably short time permeated not merely all technical but virtually all scholarly thought, and later most popular thought and day-to-day imagery as well.

So it has been for four centuries now, a remarkable synergistic combination of a creative and explanatory system of ideas with a powerful political construct and a successful economic process—each hand, if I may put it that way, washing the other. The scientific worldview has become more encompassing and pervasive with each passing generation, each passing century, and today it goes almost without challenge; indeed, we almost do not have the methods of thinking, the very language, with which to challenge it.

It shapes the patterns of our psyches and the perceptions of our senses.

It is the foundation, both practically and ideologically, of our various social systems—medicine, agriculture, communication, architecture, transportation, education, even the arts and entertainment.

It is the source and sustenance of our economy, in which we

use every scientific and technical process at our command to mold the earth's resources and terrains to human purposes, until quite recently ignorant—or scornful—of the ecological damage wrought in the extraction, conversion, use, or disposal of our treasured commodities.

It is the latticework of our political systems, West, East, and elsewhere, in which the perceived purpose of the state is to control or oversee the technologies that produce material growth and prosperity, and to accumulate the weapons that protect them.

It has become, in short, our god.

. . .

And what has been the consequence of this exchange of gods over these four centuries?

It should be said at the outset that, though some today might wish to condemn all of science as pernicious for having led us to the nuclear perils and technological mazes we now face, it cannot be so readily dismissed. The matter is too complex for that. However removed one is from the idolization of science, I think one would want to say on balance the world is a better place for our knowledge of hygiene, say, or radiotelegraphy, or immunology, or electricity, if not of nuclear fission, chemical defoliation, and psychotropic drugs. It is true that we may not have used our scientific knowledge wisely much of the time; true also that we are almost completely ignorant of the ultimate effects, either benevolent or injurious, of what we do in its name. Still, one cannot dismiss the achievements won, no matter how high the attendant price.

This cannot, however, keep us from being fully aware by now of the shortcomings, the failures, the fundamental dangers inherent in Western science; and in the death of Gaea, the transformation of our relationship to nature, we see the most threatening danger of all.

The attempt to control and manipulate nature entails severe consequences not only for the *institutions* of society—as the Frankfurt school and others have shown clearly, "domination of nature involves domination of man" (Horkheimer)—but it ultimately invites ecological disasters threatening the very *continuance* of society. The effect of scientific technology—particularly in this century of the airplane, the automobile, the satellite, the computer, and the megacity—has been to put a vast psychic distance between humans and nature, to allow people to live and work in a world in effect hermetically sealed, removed as much as possible from seeing or understanding the consequences of their actions on their environment: as, for example, the pilot in Vietnam from the defoliated countryside, the Hooker chemist from the barrels buried in Love Canal, the Ohio Valley factory owner from the dying lakes of the Adirondacks.

And there is nothing but the shortest step from this sense of separateness to the complete state of hubris that assumes that there is nothing humans can do, that science can do, that they should *not* do, because the natural world is essentially there for our benefit, our use, our comfort. The Colorado River is there to provide water for the people and farms of Southern California, needing only the technology of a Boulder Dam to complete what nature forgot to do; the Northwestern forests are there to provide lumber that the growing populations of the carelessly sprawling suburbs need to build their rightful houses; the Hudson River flows purposefully to the Atlantic so that human wastes and industrial poisons such as PCBs can be carried away, out of sight and mind, to the sea.

And if today we see the earth as a static and neutral area alterable by our chemicals and controllable by our technologies . . . if we regard ourselves as a superior species with the right to kill off as many hundreds of other species as we wish and to "have dominion over" the rest . . . if we believe we have the power to reorder nature's atoms and reassemble its genes, to contrive weapons and machines fueled by our own invented elements and capable of destroying most of life forever . . . if we create technologies capable of plundering the planet's resources, befouling its systems, poisoning its air, and altering its eons-old processes to suit our wishes . . . if this is our condition today, it is because, far from calling into question the scientific view of the universe in these last four centuries, we have in fact accepted it virtually in its entirety. We are the inevitable products of that 400-year-old experiment that has turned the world upside down—and brought it to its present crisis.

But now that we see the terrible dimensions of that crisis, now that we know our science is capable of destroying the globe in any number of ways, it is incumbent upon us to rethink our blind acceptance of that scientific view. Not that we can pretend to *eliminate* Western science somehow, to erase the scientific methods or the scientific instruments developed over the last centuries; there is no way to put the genie back in the bottle even if we wished to do so. No, the task is not to extirpate science but to incorporate it, not to dismiss it but to contain it, not to ignore its means but to question the ends to which we have put it. The task is to put its undoubtedly useful tools to work in the service of a different purpose—in the service of the preservation rather than the domination of nature.

But that sort of cognitive shift will not come easily. And the time is short.

THREE

The Crisis

IN THE LANGUAGE of ecology—a language which it behooves us all to learn—the conditions of an imperiled environment are described in a few short and pungent words:
"drawdown," "overshoot," "crash," and "die-off."

Drawdown is the process by which the dominant species in
an ecosystem uses up the surrounding resources faster than
they can be replaced and so ends up borrowing, in one form or
another, from other places and other times. For our age,
though the examples of such depletion are numerous, the
most vivid is that of fossil fuels. In the space of a little more
than a hundred years we have used up perhaps 80 percent of
the buried remains of the Carboniferous period—oil, gas, and
coal—that were deposited over a period of a hundred million
years or more, and what's more we have become totally dependent on continuing the process. One can argue about the
due-date, but the outcome is certain.

Overshoot is the inevitable and irreversible consequence of
continued drawdown, when the use of resources in an ecosystem exceeds its carrying capacity and there is no way to recover or replace what was lost. It takes many forms, depending

on the system, but perhaps the clearest and in some ways the most touching is exemplified by Easter Island. When it was first settled a thousand years ago, the island was a rich and forested land covered with palms and a small native tree called the sophora, and on its sixty-four square miles a prosperous and literate culture developed organizational and engineering skills that enabled it to erect the famous massive stone statues all along the coastline. For reasons lost in time, the population of the island over the years increased to something like 4,000 people, apparently necessitating a steady drawdown of vegetation that eventually deforested the entire island and exhausted its fertile soils. Somewhere along the line came *overshoot*, unstoppable and final, and then presumably conflict over scarce food acreage, and ultimately warfare and chaos. By the time of Captain Cook's voyage to the island in the 1770s there were barely 630 people left, eking out a marginal existence; a hundred years later, only 155 islanders remained.

Crash, as with the Easter Islanders, is what happens after overshoot—a precipitate decline in species numbers. Once a population has exceeded the capacity of its environment in one life-giving respect or another, there is no recourse, nothing to be done until that population is reduced to the level at which the resources can recover and are once again adequate to sustain it. Take the case of the famous Irish potato famine. For well over a century, year after steady year, the British encouraged and the Irish developed a near-total dependency upon a single dietary mainstay, the potato, and the population of the island grew from 2 million people to more than 8 million. Then suddenly in 1845 a natural competitor for the potato came along in the form of a parasitic fungus that got to the tubers somewhat before the people did and turned the potatoes into sticky, inedible, mucous globs. Crash: within a generation the country was devastated, more than half the population died or emigrated, and those who remained were reduced to a poverty that diminished only a century later.

Die-off and, in its final form, *die-out*, is a phenomenon common in the history of zoology and botany, and the dodo and the passenger pigeon are not exceptional. There is, for example, the everyday but suggestive experience of yeast cells introduced into a wine vat. Enormously successful as a species, they gobble up nutrients from the sugary crushed grapes around them and expand their population without a thought to the consequences of drawdown; within weeks, however, the "pollution" they produce—alcohol and carbon dioxide, which of course is what the fermentation is all about—have so filled their environment that they are unable to survive. The resulting crash, in that vat at least, means an acute die-off and then extinction.

. . .

Where along this ecological trajectory can we locate the modern—the theoretically sapient—human?

Conventional wisdom, particularly of conventional institutions and governments, has it that we are at most in a drawdown phase for a few, but hardly all, essential resources. The industrial world is indeed using fossil fuels at a prodigious rate—and, yes, zinc and manganese, and sperm whales, and groundwater, and so on and on—but there certainly seem to be adequate supplies for the near future, and in the meantime the chances are that science will come up with acceptable substitutes before any critical overshoot point is reached. Moreover the genius of modern economics is that it always provides that when commodities become scarce their price goes up, so more people will go looking for them and finding (or recycling) them in sufficient quantities. Even if supplies run low, it is hardly likely that we will have to forgo exploitation in any but a few areas, human ingenuity being what it is and past history holding true to form.

The body of ecological wisdom, however, which has been steadily and ever-more-convincingly building since the pioneering UN Conference on the Human Environment in Stockholm in 1972, suggests a good deal more caution.

Take the familiar fossil-fuels crisis for starters. If the drawdown on these fuels continues even at present rather than accelerating rates, it will deplete the world's *proven* reserves in 37 years and the *theoretically recoverable* reserves in 114 years, according to the careful Worldwatch Institute figures. And when that pinch begins it will obviously affect all aspects of an industrial world grown dependent on fossil fuelery, not just for transportation and heating but for the most basic elements of agriculture, manufacturing, and commerce, indeed the entire economic fabric. Even before the pinch, however, there could be trouble, for even as the pinch in energy supplies begins, or is perceived by market forces as likely to begin, prices will skyrocket, and as Richard Barnet argues in *The Lean Years* "a crisis of industrial civilization may well occur long before supplies are exhausted." Drawdown doesn't even have to reach overshoot, in other words, before wrenching dislocations occur. And the ramifications—as those who remember the energy shortages of the 1970s can understand—will be every bit as social and political as economic.

If one then adds other mineral resources that are being used up at a rapid pace, the full dimensions of the problem become even clearer. For the fact is that iron, bauxite, mercury, zinc, phosphate, chromite, manganese, cadmium, uranium, tin, tungsten, and maybe copper and lead are *all* expected (even by optimistic industry sources) to be exhausted within forty years, even at present (not exponential) rates of use.

Depending for a way out on science, the very tool that has enabled us to find and use up all these resources so efficiently in so short a time, seems quite misplaced, simply as a matter of logic. Perhaps it is misplaced also as a matter of fact, there being general agreement in the scientific world that the period of invention is probably winding down, and the task for the near future is largely to refine existing ideas and technologies rather than create new ones. But even if science is as wondrous in the next half-century as it has been in the past, it will still face the seemingly insuperable task of finding substitutes for all the above resources, and fairly quickly—substitutes, of course, which will have to be economical, efficient, abundant, and pollution-free. And it will have to do this without creating *new* problems, a facility it has so far been notoriously short of; as David Ehrenfeld, a professor of biology at Rutgers University and a long-time ecologist, writes in his comprehensive *Conserving Life on Earth*: "Science and technology have a long history of creating ecological problems; their record for solutions that do not in themselves generate more problems is less than impressive."

Depending on a benign economy, as many conservative thinkers of the Herman Kahn ilk would do, seems hardly better placed, especially since the economy is *based* precisely on the concepts of exploitation, productivity, and growth. It is no doubt true that, as drawdown continues, the price of the depleted commodities will increase, and so eventually suppliers will find it "economical" to work more difficult terrains and recover more low-quality ores. Yet that fails to confront the fact that, even then, there are finite limits of these resources; nothing in the holy ark of any religion says the gods were supposed to have stocked the earth with caches of bauxite and zinc that would never run out. It also fails to consider that the process of recovering ever-scarcer resources in ever-more-remote terrains necessarily increases both energy costs, which may well rise far faster than the price of the commodity itself, and environmental risks, which may well be expensive to guard against or simply intolerable for societies to permit.

Counting on conservation seems similarly misplaced. Although the international industrial system can moderate the use of some resources, it is geared to a geometric growth that simply does not permit stasis and equilibrium.* The system can grow for a while by emphasizing conservation-oriented industries such as recycling, but in the end the demands of geometric growth will outstrip resources. Besides, recycling cannot reclaim materials that are destroyed in the process of use, such as gasoline, or that are incorporated into products or structures that will endure for a long time.

The somber ecological view, therefore, is that our overall drawdown of resources has reached a critical point and, for many valuable commodities, may have reached the point of overshoot. But there are other forms of drawdown, too, in the contemporary world, some more subtle:

· Industrialized agriculture is in its fourth decade of reckless and widespread drawdown of soil, water, and minerals, which has so depleted the earth's richness that it is now maintained only by the use of extremely large quantities of fossil fuels, chemical fertilizers, and pesticides.

· The drawdown of groundwater and overuse of fragile ecosystems, usually by overgrazing, have created deserts throughout the world—the UN says that by 1982 about 65 percent of once-arable land had become dry, barren, and un-

*Although conservation of a sort was forced on oil consumption, the world today is still using just as much as it did ten years ago when the conservation effort began, and its consumption of fossil fuels of all kinds has gone on increasing at the usual exponential rates.

usable—and contributed to the decline in worldwide food production that will be epidemic early in the twenty-first century.

· A drawdown of our fellow species, both intended (ocean fishing, fur trapping) and unintended (pollution, dam construction), is causing them to become extinct at a rate estimated to be a thousand times faster than during even the most destructive periods of the geological past.

· Worldwide urbanization continues at an alarming rate everywhere, everywhere creating huge populations that live far beyond the carrying capacities of their own territory and that depend on massive drawdowns of food, water, and commodities from other regions.

· The drawdown of forests, particularly tropical rainforests, has already disrupted the vital "breathing" function of worldwide photosynthesis and may have overshot the earth's ability to restore enough carbon monoxide to the atmosphere.

· What is in effect a drawdown of the earth's cleansing and waste-storage capacity has severely threatened the pollution tolerance of air, land, and water around the world and in many places has obviously overshot those limits, perhaps irremediably.

· And it is even possible that the cumulative drawdown effects of industrial civilization have already transformed patterns of weather and climate beyond recovery, forcing radical alterations of human settlement and behavior, if they permit survival at all.

Ecological opinion based upon such dire considerations as these is necessarily gloomy—and as I read through the bulk of the literature I find a general sentiment that, if we are to escape global disaster on a large scale, we do not have much time to make the necessary changes. All too typical is this conclusion from a group of scientists at a Massachusetts Institute of Technology conference, a Study of Critical Environmental Problems:

> The risk is very great that we shall overshoot in our environmental demands (as some ecologists claim we have already done), leading to cumulative collapse of our civilization. It seems obvious that before the end of the century we must accomplish basic changes in our relations with ourselves and with nature. If this is to be done, we must begin now.

Or ecologist David Ehrenfeld:

> Mankind has begun to experience locally the first warning signs and symptoms of a global ecological deterioration. . . . By economies and substitutions combined with new prospecting and mining techniques we ought to be able to postpone the inevitable raw materials crisis at least until the end of the twentieth century. In the case of the destruction of the natural world, the period of grace seems shorter and the prospects more gloomy.

Or, finally, the conclusions of a far-from-alarmist scholar like Gary Coates of Kansas State University, editor of the comprehensive *Resettling America: Energy, Ecology, and Community*:

> Industrial civilization will be forced to make a rapid transition from its current business-as-usual growth ethic to a steady-state society. . . . [This] great cultural transformation must be effectively completed within the next 50 to 100 years. If it is not, we shall experience this turning point in history as the

31

greatest period of violence, suffering, and destruction ever known.

And he then adds this doomsday caution:

Even if we are able to begin reversing current trends today, we shall not be able to escape the disorientation, confusion, and suffering implied by such an unprecedented cultural change.

• • •

As pessimistic and depressing as these experts and their numerous colleagues may be (and I could quote hundreds like them), they are still able to imagine the human species in the late-drawdown—or should I say early-overshoot?—stage. Others argue, far more frighteningly, that we are unknowingly already in the first throes of crash.

William Catton, for example, a professor of sociology at Washington State University and author of an extremely sobering book of ecological analysis called *Overshoot*, argues flatly that our species has expanded so copiously and used resources so prodigiously that "now we must expect crash": "Nature must, in the not far distant future, institute bankruptcy proceedings against industrial civilization, and perhaps against the standing crop of human flesh, just as nature had done many times to other detritus-consuming species following their exuberant expansion."

According to Catton's "most realistic" model of our ecological paths, industrialism's drawdown load has *already* exceeded the carrying capacity of the earth—even the capacity as augmented during the past century by all the ingenuity of our technological system—and all we can expect in the near future is more of the same: more drawdown and less capacity until, finally, crash—a crash, he argues, from which the human race might never recover. "Having become a species of superdetritovores"—living off dead matter such as the fossil fuels in great extravagance—"mankind was destined not merely for succession, but for crash."

To take only one example supporting this conclusion, Catton suggests that our drawdown of fossil fuels, apart from all its other pernicious consequences, is ultimately changing the balance of oxygen and carbon that makes life on earth possible for respiratory animals. "Hundreds of millions of years of evolution," he writes, "had produced the oxygen-rich and nearly carbon-free atmosphere we need," and now "mankind seemed bent on undoing in just a few centuries what nature had so slowly accomplished." We are bringing to the surface the carbon that nature had buried safely under the earth's crust and putting it into the air, and at some not-too-distant point we will discover that it is starting to overwhelm the oxygen content; already the carbon dioxide levels in the atmosphere have increased dramatically in recent decades (and by more than 40 percent over the last century). At the same time, by cutting down the world's forests—half the trees on the planet in 1950 have been felled today—we have removed those very life forms that could absorb atmospheric carbon through photosynthesis.

That is what leads Catton to say, near the end of his book:

These final chapters provide no magic recipe for avoiding crash. There is none, when overshoot has already happened. It is in acknowledging that unwelcome fact that this book differs most fundamentally from previous ecological analyses.

Catton is not alone. John Hamaker also predicts ecological disaster for *Homo industrialus*. An engineer by profession and an ecologist by persuasion, Hamaker is the author of a dense and thoroughly documented book, *The Survival of Civilization*, which in point of fact offers very little hope in that direction. In Hamaker's view we are about to be victims of a new ice age that will totally transform the agricultural patterns of the globe: "Hard evidence insures that by 1995 the temperate zone will become a subarctic zone and the world will have lost its food supply."

That hard evidence begins with the paleobotanical and geological findings that ice ages have recurred on earth approximately every 90,000 years or so, and that it is now just about that long since the last one. This natural cycle, however, has been severely exacerbated by the various human drawdowns that have severely stressed the earth's systems, two in particular. First, soils exhausted and demineralized by industrial farming, engineered drainage systems, overbuilding, and overpopulation now support only a fragile plant and forest cover ever more susceptible to disease, acid rain, fire, and insects. Second, the overuse of fossil fuels has greatly increased atmospheric carbon dioxide, which the weakened forests can no longer absorb as they once could, and in fact they are giving up their own natural carbons to the air at a rate that accelerates every year.

Together these two processes produce an inevitable third: the famous "greenhouse effect" in the tropics, where the increased carbon dioxide traps the sun's heat, raises temperatures markedly, and (according to Hamaker) generates a concomitant huge, ever-moist cloud cover at the poles that will continuously drop snow and keep the coldest regions shaded from the sun. The result, within a decade, will be an ice age whose consequences will be truly devastating.

The glaciation itself is not the threat—it will not reach as far south as the United States for perhaps 40,000 years—but rather the combination of climatic events leading up to that: forests in the temperate climes dying with increased acidification, demineralization, drought, and fire; temperate farm-

34

lands depleted from these and other causes, particularly temperature changes that will make most of the world's grainbelt too cold for cereal crops; in the tropics, cropland being depleted by drought, overheating, and overuse; wind velocities increasing to 100 miles an hour or more as climatic conditions sharpen, with further depletion of cropland and forest soils; additional volcanoes erupting everywhere (and therefore *more* carbon dioxide) due to added pressure on the earth's crust from the added polar ice; and water shortages desiccating both tropic and temperate latitudes.

In Hamaker's vision:

Drought, which is normal to glaciation, . . . now joins soil acidification to kill all the temperate zone vegetation. The forests will go up in flames. . . . By the year 2000 the carbon dioxide will have jumped at least 100 ppm [parts per million]. The North Pole ice field will expand very rapidly. Winter storms will be brutal and summers short, hot, and dry. Spring and fall will bring massive floods.

Unless something is done, and immediately, Hamaker says, "civilization will be dead."

It would be comforting to dismiss Hamaker's doom-and-gloom, except that, sadly, there are a good many pieces of evidence to support it. Earthquake activity is in fact increasing, and in the 1970s and '80s was nearly ten times as great as in the 1920s and '30s. . . . Volcanic activity has increased by a surprising 5 percent a year throughout the last decade. . . . Polar glaciers are growing larger, steadily advancing southward since 1953; the polar dust load has grown by a factor of 100 since the 1950s. . . . Toxic pollution from both volcanoes and humans is increasing in intensity and extent, and new evidence of weakened forest stands now comes not only from the Adirondacks and Canada, long known to be victimized, but from the Green Mountains, the Appalachians, the southern pine forests, and from throughout northern Europe. . . . Soil erosion is already reported at record rates in many parts of the US, and topsoil is being depleted in temperate zones world-wide by an estimated 23 billion tons a year, an unprecedented toll. . . . Desertification has increased on all continents, most sharply and poignantly in Africa but noticeably also in North America, particularly in the American Southwest and Mexico. . . .

It is enough to give a person an apocalyptic sense, even if this or that finding is to be discounted, or ignored, or disbe-lieved. Not surprising that Hamaker, compiling such data, was moved to tell his scientific colleagues:

> Take a hard look at where we are in 1984, 18,000 years into the climate cycle. It is a picture of the death of civilization within this decade. Don't look for the creator to save us—he designed it to work this way. If we are too stupid, too greedy, too uncivilized to pull together to solve our problems, then so be it—we die.

Die-off—and perhaps die-out?

• • •

I will not side myself with the voices of doom.

I do not know where along the slide from drawdown to die-off the human species may now have located itself, and I can-not fail to be impressed by the weight of evidence showing that it is well along toward the latter. Certainly it would be foolish to deny the mounting evidence that an ecological crisis of some magnitude seems to be at hand. Sometimes it is com-forting to quibble with this figure or that assumption or those lines of reasoning, to locate a contrary source, a different ex-pert, to denigrate one professor's credentials, another's research techniques. But there is simply no escaping the rock-hard truths of the overall evidence of environmental peril in which our human society has plunged itself.

Still. Still, I cannot think that a species bent upon suicide and ecocide cannot be *forced* to see its own calamitous path before it is too late, simply by the processes of self-preservation that must abide within it. Believing in Gaea, I believe that it is in her interests to try to keep most of the major living species on her crust from destroying themselves. In the human species she has found an exceedingly skillful, adaptive, intelligent organism capable of great creativity and productivity, capable of the specialized functions of heightened multisense perception and language-based memory, a unique animal to receive and store the planet's information. I think in some sense our survival is useful to her.

Well, yes, the dinosaurs. But I am stubborn. I now choose to believe that their extinction had nothing to do with their inability to adapt to new climates or new competitors but was rather caused by those bombardments of meteors that some people say saturated the earth those many millions of years ago. Something *done to* Gaea, that is, rather than something she did.

Facing the evidence of our ecological insanity, I take what little comfort I can from the thought that, somehow, we are useful, and from the belief that we have at our grasp the instrument—the philosophy, if you will—by which to begin to rescue, even now, our beleaguered species, creating for ourselves before it is too late an ecological worldview with which to replace the scientific worldview—perhaps more accurately described by now as an *industrio*-scientific worldview—that has so imperiled us.

That instrument, that philosophy, is the bioregional vision.

II

The Bioregional Paradigm

We shall not cease from exploration
And the end of all our exploring
Will be to arrive where we started
And know the place for the first time.
T. S. Eliot, "Little Gidding"

A region holds the power to sustain and join disparate people:
old ground charged with common wholeness and forces of
long-growing life. All people are within regions as a condition
of existence, and regions condition all people within them.
Peter Berg, "Amble Toward Continent Congress"

FOUR

Dwellers in the Land

In *The Interpreters*, a book written at the height of the Irish Revolution by the Irish author known as AE, there is a passage in which a group of prisoners, a disparate lot, sit around discussing what the ideal new world should look like. One of them, a philosopher, advances the now-familiar vision of a unitary world order with a global, scientific, cosmopolitan culture. Another, the poet Lavelle, argues fervently against this conception, trying to show that the more the world develops its technological superstructure, the farther it gets from its natural roots. "If all wisdom was acquired from without," he says, "it might be politic for us to make our culture cosmopolitan. But I believe our best wisdom does not come from without, but arises in the soul and is an emanation of the Earth spirit, a voice speaking directly to us dwellers in this land."

It is not difficult to imagine the alternative to the peril the industrio-scientific paradigm has placed us in. It is simply to become "dwellers in the land."

We must try to regain the spirit of the ancient Greeks, once again comprehending the earth as a living creature and contriving the modern equivalent of the worship of Gaea. We must try to learn that she is, in every real sense, *sacred*, and that there is therefore a holy way to confront her and her works, a way of awe and admiration and respect and veneration that simply will not permit despoliation or abuse. We must try to understand ourselves as participants in and not masters over her biotic community—a "reinvention of the human at the species level," in the philosopher Thomas Berry's telling phrase—and take to heart Mark Twain's remark that humans are different from other animals only in that they are able to blush—or need to.

But to become dwellers in the land, to relearn the laws of Gaea, to come to know the earth fully and honestly, the crucial and perhaps only and all-encompassing task is to understand *place*, the immediate specific place where we live. The kinds of soils and rocks under our feet; the source of the waters we drink; the meaning of the different kinds of winds; the common insects, birds, mammals, plants, and trees; the particular cycles of the seasons; the times to plant and harvest and forage—these are the things that are necessary to know. The limits of its resources; the carrying capacities of its lands and waters; the places where it must not be stressed; the places where its bounties can best be developed; the treasures it holds and the treasures it withholds—these are the things that must be understood. And the cultures of the people, of the populations native to the land and of those who have grown up with it, the human social and economic arrangements shaped by and adapted to the geomorphic ones, in both urban and rural settings—these are the things that must be appreciated.

That, in essence, is *bioregionalism*.

Now I would be the last to say that the word "bioregionalism" is one that comes easily to the lips; indeed, let's face it, it is a clumsy word, and difficult, and not only because most people do not instantly grasp a meaning for it. But I believe it to be a concept so accessible and, once understood, so serviceable and even productive, that it is worthwhile using it and explaining its meaning over time.

There is nothing so mysterious about the elements of the word, after all—*bio* is from the Greek word for forms of life, as in *biology* and *biography*, and *region* is from the Latin *regere*, territory to be ruled—and there is nothing, after a moment's thought, so terribly difficult in what they convey together: a life-territory, a place defined by its life forms, its topography and its biota, rather than by human dictates; a region governed by nature, not legislature. And if the concept initially strikes us as strange, that may perhaps only be a measure of how distant we have become from the wisdom it conveys—and how badly we need that wisdom now.

There is another cogent reason for using this word. Since it was first propagated by writer Peter Berg and ecologist Raymond Dasmann more than a decade ago—it is not quite clear who originated the term, but it was those two, working through an organization called Planet Drum and a newspaper irreverently called *Raise the Stakes*, who brought the concept to a wider audience—it has inspired what can fairly be called a movement, albeit still a modest one. As of 1985 there were some sixty groups in North America specifically defining themselves as bioregional, and a nascent continental organization, the North American Bioregional Congress, formed to advance bioregional consciousness and to nurture and link bioregional organizations. Those developments give the word a sufficient lineage, a sufficient currency, to justify its being honored by further usage.

· · ·

Bioregionalism will define itself more completely in the course of all that follows, but initially it ought to be helpful to get a sense, a feel, of the concept by following some of its natural implications.

Knowing the land. We may not become as sophisticated about the land we live upon and its resources as the original inhabitants, those who had forty words for snow or knew every tree in the forest. But any one of us can walk the territory and see what inhabits there, become conscious of the birdsongs and waterfalls and animal droppings, follow a brooklet to a stream and down to a river, and learn when to set out tomatoes, what kind of soil is best for celery, and where blueberries thrive. On a more sophisticated level, we can develop a resource inventory for the region, using information from the local Forest Service to map and count the area's trees; checking hydrological surveys to determine waterflows, runoffs, and hydropower sites; collecting biological profiles of the native annual and perennial food plants; learning annual climatic conditions and the full potentials of solar, wind, and water power; and studying human land-use patterns and optimal settlement areas. Out of all that—much of it already available, though not broken down on a bioregional basis—one could ultimately determine with some grandeur the carrying capacity of the region.

Now that does sound a bit bucolic, I realize, and it may be hard to see immediately how it translates into urban terms.* But every city is part of a region, after all, and depends on the surrounding countryside for many of its resources and much

---

*It may be worthwhile to dispel the myth, propagated by the Census Bureau and others, that this nation is predominantly urban: it is in fact largely *non*-urban and getting more so. About two-thirds of the population lives outside even modest cities (50,000 and up), more than a third of that in rural areas and unincorporated villages. Even in so-called "metropolitan areas" some 40 percent of the people live outside the cities proper.

of its market, and every city is built upon a natural foundation. Knowing place for the urban-dweller, then, means learning the details of the trade and resource-dependency between city and country and the population limits appropriate to the region's carrying capacity. It also suggests exploring the natural *potential* of the land on which the city rests—for though our huge conurbations have largely displaced natural life by diverting rivers, cutting down forests, paving over soils, and confining most animal life to zoos and parks, it is also true that one can discover and measure the possibilities for rooftop gardens, solar energy, recycling, urban silviculture, and the like.

Learning the lore. Every place has a history, a record of how both the human and natural possibilities of the region have been explored, and this must be studied with new eyes: there is more to discover, as botanist Wes Jackson puts it, than to invent. And though not every place has kept its history properly alive, a fountain of information still exists if we will but tap it—as shown, for example, in the wonderful Foxfire books, the recent collections of Indian lore, and many other projects of oral history and folk knowledge.

Obviously we will not want—or be able—to live as the ancients did. But every serious historical and anthropological exploration of their ways and wisdom shows that earlier cultures, particularly those well-rooted in the earth, knew a number of important things we are only now learning about: the value of herbal medicines, for example, or methods and times of burning prairie grassland, or siting and building houses for maximum passive-solar effect, or the regular and central role of women in tribal decision-making. If nothing else, such history helps us realize that the past was not as bleak and laborious and unhealthy as the high-energy-high-tech proponents try to make out. It was E. F. Schumacher who re-

45

minded us that when the modern world organized its thinking "by some extraordinary structure we call objective science," it discarded the "two great teachers" of humanity: "the marvelous system of living nature" and "the traditional wisdom of mankind" by which we know about it. It seems high time to rectify the balance.

Developing the potential. Once the place and its possibilities are known, the bioregional task is to see how this potential can best be realized *within* the boundaries of the region, using all the biotic and geological resources to their fullest, constrained only by the logic of necessity and the principles of ecology. Fully developing the bioregion allows the full development of the people and communities within it, each section of it able to employ long-neglected processes and long-unused ingenuity but with the full blessing of contemporary knowledge and skills.

Self-reliance, not so much at the individual as at the regional level, is thus inherent in the bioregional concept. We might begin to think of how much of any region's human and material resources are ignored or squandered or left undeveloped because the region looks to far-off sources and depends on extrinsic goods and services instead. We might look at how much of a region's wealth is exported to distant banks or home-offices or absentee owners, instead of watering the gardens at home. And we might try to imagine just what could be done in any region if all its funds, facilities, stocks, and talents were used to their fullest, limited only by the carrying capacity of the land and its ecological constraints.

Liberating the self. Bioregionalism implies also the development of individual potential within the development of the region, along two broad perspectives.

On the one hand, many present constraints on personal freedom and choice from without would be diminished or eliminated—those of distant and impersonal market forces, for example, remote governments and bureaucracies, and unseen corporations dictating consumer choices—while within the bioregion both economic and political opportunities would be inevitably opened up. Also, by living closer to the land one necessarily lives closer to the community, able to enjoy the communitarian values of cooperation, participation, sodality, and reciprocity that enhance individual development.

On the other hand, fully knowing the character of the natural world and being connected to it in a daily and physical way provides that sense of oneness, of *rootedness* that the ancients experienced—and "to be rooted," as philosopher Simone Weil was shrewd enough to know, "is perhaps the most important and least recognized need of the human soul." Moreover, it seems clear from the past that individuals who can best use, because they best understand, the gifts of nature—for food, for energy, for shelter, for crafts—are able to develop and prosper in ways unavailable to those who lack those skills.

Knowing, learning, developing, liberating—these, then, are some of the processes most central to the bioregional idea. Their implications are elaborate and far-reaching, as we shall explore in the chapters that follow.

• • •

Obviously, bioregionalism is at once very simple and very complicated.

Very simple, because all of its components are *there*, unhidden, right around us, right where we live; because we know that other people, ancient and in our terms perhaps unsophisticated, understood these things and lived for uncomplicated centuries by them. To discover and present the kind of information basic to a bioregional society is not difficult. There are still many old people among us today who know some of the wisdom of our forebears, and the discipline of modern ecology uses contemporary scientific procedures that can help us construct the rest of the bioregional body of knowledge.

Very complicated, because it is so at odds with the conventional way of looking at the world nowadays that it must strike most people at first as either too limiting and provincial, or quaintly nostalgic, or wide-eyed and utopian, or simply irrelevant—or all of those. That is hardly surprising, and the difficulties must be faced frankly.

Obviously it will take a considerable change in attitude before our industrial society begins first to abandon the notion of controlling and remaking the world in the name of a global monoculture and then to realize that maybe what it calls "provincial" is merely the kind of minding-your-own-business attention to local reforms within the limits of the possible that might have a chance of saving the world.

It will take some time before people recognize that the project of understanding place is neither nostalgic nor utopian but rather the realistic sort of occupation anyone can participate in every day that has an immediate and practical chance of curbing our present waste and recklessness.

It will take some broad and persuasive education to get people to realize that it is not the bioregional task that is irrelevant but precisely the business-as-usual politics of *all* the major parties of *all* the major industrial nations, not one of which has made ecological salvation a significant priority, not one of which is prepared to abandon or even curtail the industrial economy that is imperiling us.

And it will take patience to lead people past their fear and lingering hatred of the natural world, which grows as their ignorance of it grows, and on to appreciation of Gaea as a precious living entity that acts always in reasonable homeostatic ways, violently at times, and unpredictably at times, but for an ultimately benevolent and life-sustaining purpose.*

Please understand: I do not underestimate the complications. Yet I am certain that in the bioregional paradigm we have a goal, a philosophy, and a process by which to create a world which is not only *necessary* for the continuation of our species, but is also *desirable* and *possible*.

• • •

The first of all of Gaea's daughters was Themis, to whom she entrusted the laws of nature, and it is in the diligent study of those laws that we can best guide ourselves in reconstructing human societies for a bioregional world. To be sure, the laws of nature can sometimes seem confusing and indeed contradictory, and even experts who have spent lifetimes on this sort of work have not always come to the same conclusions. We would be well advised to approach the job with caution.

But after a fairly extensive reading of the literature here, I am struck by what seems to be a wide agreement at least to the broad outlines of what Gaea's laws are and the general directions they suggest for human settlements and systems. I am struck, too, by the extreme variety of the investigators who have arrived at such similar conclusions: ecologists and

*Just as a single example of popular fear of the natural, Dr. Lewis Thomas mentions the common paranoia about diseases and bacteria in this society, where we think "we live in a world where the microbes are always trying to get at us, to tear us cell from cell, and we only stay alive and whole through diligence and fear." Actually, he points out, disease and pathogenicity "is not the rule" in nature and indeed "occurs so infrequently and involves such a relatively small number of species, considering the huge population of bacteria on the earth, that it has a freakish aspect."

architects, political scientists and economists, sociologists and naturalists, writers and planners, some carefully "without politics," some frankly conservative, many no more than liberal, and a few forthrightly decentralist and regionalist. I think it is possible to deduce from their work over these past several generations the central principles by which to construct the guiding tenets of an ecological world: the *bioregional paradigm*.

Such a paradigm of course stands in sharp contrast to the industrio-scientific paradigm in almost every aspect. I will examine it in some detail throughout this section, but it might be useful at the start to compare those paradigms and see their differences starkly:

	BIOREGIONAL PARADIGM	INDUSTRIO-SCIENTIFIC PARADIGM
Scale	Region	State
	Community	Nation/World
Economy	Conservation	Exploitation
	Stability	Change/Progress
	Self-sufficiency	World Economy
	Cooperation	Competition
Polity	Decentralization	Centralization
	Complementarity	Hierarchy
	Diversity	Uniformity
Society	Symbiosis	Polarization
	Evolution	Growth/Violence
	Division	Monoculture

There are great complexities here, of course, and overlaps and interconnections that such a chart tends to disguise. In the following pages I will try to develop and examine these concepts and their linkages more carefully, approaching them in the order the chart suggests, focusing on the four basic determinants of any organized civilization: scale, economy, polity, and society. And thus I hope to portray in the round the bioregional paradigm, the means by which we may become "dwellers in the land."

FIVE

Scale

NOT LONG AGO I was invited by the philosophy department of a major university to participate in a symposium on "Ethical Responses to Environmental Threats," or something of that sort, during which I was forced to sit through several long and tedious papers about the correct moral responses to world hunger and endangered species and resource depletion and the like. I could see that a good many people in the audience were as bewildered as I was by these talks, and in the question period several of them challenged the speakers: how can you expect people to be *moral*, the tenor of their responses went, about something that most of them don't understand as having very much connection with their lives and can't see their individual behavior as having any effect on? What, after all, is supposed to be my "ethical response" to Japan's harvesting of the endangered beluga whale, even if I happen to know about it—what's it got to do with morality, anyway? Am I more or less moral if I feel bad, or protest, or boycott Toyotas, and just what difference could that make to the Japanese fishing industry? Are *they* supposed to have some "ethical response" to their profession, and can they be expected to see the moral component in saving the animal they are supposed to hunt? And why do environmental problems of any kind call for an *ethical* stance when they seem to involve purely practical questions of, for example, getting more food to starving people or developing more solar energy devices to replace fossil fuels?

The challenged panelists seemed baffled by this response. They frowned and smiled and went back to their previous "oughts" and "shoulds" and "right behaviors": if it is "wrong" to kill endangered species or pollute the atmosphere, then people should not do it and should be *taught* not to do it because it's a moral transgression. Most of the audience remained unconvinced.

At this point, perhaps recklessly, I chose to intervene. The issue is not one of morality, I said, but of *scale*. There is no very successful way to teach, or force, the moral view, or to insure correct ethical responses to anything at all. The only way people will apply "right behavior" and behave in a responsible way is if they have been persuaded to see the problem concretely and to understand their own connections to it directly—and this can be done only at a limited scale. It can be done where the forces of government and society are still recognizable and comprehensible, where relations with other people are still intimate, and where the effects of individual actions are visible; where abstractions and intangibles give way to the here and now, the seen and felt, the real and known. Then people will do the environmentally "correct" thing not because it is thought to be the *moral*, but rather the *practical*, thing to do. That cannot be done on a global scale, nor a continental, nor even a national one, because the human animal, being small and limited, has only a small view of the world and a limited comprehension of how to act within it.

Scale, in other words, I said, solves many of the abstract and theoretical problems the philosophers dither themselves into knots over. It specifically solves the problem of "responses to environmental threats" so that this is no longer a rarefied academic issue. For if there is any scale at which ecological consciousness can be developed, at which citizens can see themselves as being the *cause* for the environmental *effect*, it is at the regional level; there all ecological questions are taken out of the realm of the philosophical and the moral and are dealt with as immediate and personal. People do not, other things being equal, pollute and damage those natural systems on which they depend for life and livelihood if they see directly what is happening; nor voluntarily use up a resource under their feet and before their eyes if they perceive that it is precious, needed, vital; nor kill off species they can see are important for the smooth functioning of the ecosystem. When they look with Gaean eyes and feel a Gaean consciousness, as they can at the bioregional scale, there is no longer any need to worry about the abstruse effluvia of "ethical responses" to the world around.*

So if I begin this discussion of the bioregional paradigm with the concept of scale it is because I believe it to be, at bottom, the single critical and decisive determinant of all human constructs, be they buildings, systems, or societies. No work of human ingenuity, however perfect otherwise, can possibly

---

*I know there are people who appear to be destroying their own environments voluntarily—the Japanese whalers who deplete the oceans of the very animals they need to survive on, the wheat farmers over the Ogallala aquifer who use up the very groundwater they need to sustain their farms, and others who live out the short-term parable that Garrett Hardin has described as "the tragedy of the commons." But these people do not live at a bioregional scale. They think of the world not in ecological but in economic terms and are usually in service to distant economic forces that have no regard for their particular environment, so they are in fact happy to use it up for their immediate financial gains no matter what the long-term destruction may be.

be successful if it is too small or, more to the usual point, too big, just as a door fails if it is too small to get through, a doorknob if it is too large to grasp; just as an economy fails if it is too small to provide shelter as well as food, a government if it is too large to let all its citizens know about and regularly influence its actions.

At the right scale human potential is unleashed, human comprehension magnified, human accomplishment multiplied. I would argue that the optimum scale is the bioregional, not so small as to be powerless and impoverished, not so large as to be ponderous and impervious, a scale at which at last human potential can match ecological reality.

· · ·

In reading Gaea's laws it is of course difficult to establish primacy, but it is probably not far wrong to suggest that, where scale is concerned, the first law is that the face of the earth is organized not into artificial states but natural regions, and those regions, while varying greatly in size, are mostly much more limited than those defined by national boundaries.

The natural region is the bioregion, defined by the qualities Gaea has established there, the *givens* of nature. It is any part of the earth's surface whose rough boundaries are determined by natural characteristics rather than human dictates, distinguishable from other areas by particular attributes of flora, fauna, water, climate, soils, and landforms, and by the human settlements and cultures those attributes have given rise to. The borders between such areas are usually not rigid—nature works of course with flexibility and fluidity—but the general contours of the regions themselves are not hard to identify by using a little ecological knowledge. Indeed, those contours are generally felt, understood, or in some way sensed, by many of the inhabitants of the area, particularly those closest to the land—farmers, ranchers, hunters, hikers, fishers, foresters, ecologists, botanists, and most especially (for America) the tribal Indians still in touch with their ancient cultures that for centuries knew the earth as sacred and its wellbeing as imperative.

One rather interesting thing about the bioregional perspective is that through a close analysis of nature's patterns—in maps of physiographic provinces and natural vegetation and soil distribution and forest belts and climatic types and riverine systems and land-use variations and all the other natural features the experts have diligently charted—you begin to see something almost (appropriately enough) organic. For it turns out that bioregions are not only of different sizes but often can be seen to be like Chinese boxes, one within another, forming a complex arrangement from the largest to the smallest, depending upon which natural characteristics are dominant.

The whole matter is complex, but we can get a general idea of this fascinating structural pattern if we start by looking at the largest sort of bioregion and move toward the smaller.

Ecoregion. The widest natural region, taking its character from the broadest distribution of native vegetation and soil types, might be called the ecoregion. It is a huge area of perhaps several hundred thousand square miles, normally (in the American setting) covering several states, its outlines determined largely by the spread of its trees or grasses at the time when its natural development was at its *climax* phase of maturity and stability. The boundaries are likely to be most imprecise at this stage, but one can identify about forty such ecoregions across the North American continent.

The Ozark Plateau is a good example. It covers some 55,000 square miles clearly demarcated by the Missouri, Mississippi, and Arkansas rivers, uplifted in a dome some 2,000 feet above the surrounding terrain. Its natural forest of predominantly oak and hickory is distinguishable from the pine forests to the south and the tall-grass prairie to the west, and its calcareous and chert soils are distinct from the non-calcareous deposits to the east and the sandstones and shales to the south and west. Or take the Sonoran Desert, that arid, scrub-brush area of perhaps 100,000 square miles that stretches from the southern foothills of the Sierra Nevada and the Mojave Desert down along the Gulf of California to the Sonora River and the northern edges of the Sinaloan forest. It is distinct in vegetation as the province of the creosote bush, saguaro and cardon cacti, jojoba, ironwood, and white bursage; in native animal life as the territory of bighorn sheep, pronghorns, and Gambel's quail; in climate as a hot, dry land of double cycles of rain and drought each year.

Georegion. Within the large ecoregion it is possible to distinguish smaller bioregions with their own coherent characteristics, identified most often by clear physiographic features such as river basins, valleys, and mountain ranges, and often some special floral and faunal traits as well. A watershed—the flows and valleys of a major river system—is a particularly distinctive kind of georegion, more easily mapped than most, with aquatic and riverine life usually quite special to that area and with human settlements and economies peculiar to that river.

Within the Ozark ecoregion, for example, the White River watershed forms a discrete georegion easily visible from the air, and much of the biota around its major lakes—Beaver, Table Rock, Bull Shoals, Norfolk—can be differentiated, though sometimes in only marginal ways, from the rest of the ecoregion. The Central Valley of California forms another readily visible georegion within a Northern California ecoregion. It is a lush stretch of 20,000 square miles or so along the Sacramento and San Joaquin rivers, whose native wildlife before the dominance of agribusiness included ducks, geese, swans, tule elk, condors, coyote, grizzly bears, and antelope, a mix celebrated by the Indian tribes of the region exactly because of its distinctiveness; and whose vegetation and climate make it quite different from the coastal forests, Sierra foothills, and Klamath Mountains with which it shares the ecoregion.

Morphoregion. Finally, in some places, the georegions break down into a series of smaller territories of perhaps several thousand square miles, identifiable by distinctive life forms on the surface—towns and cities, mines and factories, fields and farms—and the special land forms that gave rise to those particular features in the first place. A watershed, for example, will often change its character perceptibly as it flows from its headwaters to its mouth; with it change the kinds of human activities that accompany the river on its journey and thus the varying styles of human culture and agriculture along the way.

The Connecticut River Basin, to take an obvious example, is a long and fertile georegion running between the Green and the White mountains all the way from Canada down to the Long Island Sound. Although it is obviously a coherent watershed, it undergoes several evident changes: in the north, cutting through the hilly country of Vermont and New Hampshire, it is mostly pinched and narrow with the forest vegetation very near the water's edge and the human settlements small and far between; when the valley broadens out below the Deerfield River, in Massachusetts, the hills and forests recede and dairy, tobacco, and vegetable farms spread out on both sides of the river, with several sizeable cities along the way; finally, as it reaches the solid and resistant Meshomasic foothills around Middletown, the river takes on a sylvan look again, with steeper slopes, so there are few human settlements until the saltwater towns around Saybrook Harbor.

. . .

Obviously this business of bioregional identification is no simple matter, but the broad distinctions are clear enough to anyone who will look—one cannot mistake the Sonoran Desert nor the Ozark Plateau—and probably at this stage of bioregional development it is more important to appreciate these general contours, the rough outlines of the Gaean design, than worry overmuch about elaborate and immutable delineations. The borders will almost always be indistinct in any case, because we are dealing with the soft and flexible ways of nature; nothing will tell the yarrow or the chigger where the exact boundaries of the Ozark Plateau are to be, nothing confine the lovely phainopepla to the precise borders of the Sonoran lowlands. There is an advantage in keeping borders vague, even if it goes against the scientistic love of fixedness, for it tends to encourage a blend, a cross-fertilization of cultures at the bioregional edges, to blunt the possessiveness and defensiveness that rigid borders so often cause, and to keep in check the human propensity to stamp our lines and purposes on nature's.

Moreover, ultimately the task of determining the appropriate bioregional boundaries—and how seriously to take them—will always be left up to the inhabitants of the area, the dwellers in the land, who will always know them best. It turns out not to be all that esoteric a process, in fact sufficiently comprehensible to have been a common part of the way most preliterate societies close to the soil ordered themselves.

One can see this fairly clearly in the case of the Indian peoples who first settled the North American continent. Because they had to live off the land, and because their styles of living varied according to the styles of the land, they distributed themselves to a remarkable degree along the lines of what we now recognize as bioregions.

Take, for example, the tribal conglomeration of Algonkian-speaking peoples along the Eastern seaboard. Before the arrival of European invaders, they settled over a territory stretching from somewhere near the Gulf of St. Lawrence down to the Chesapeake Bay—very nearly what a bioregionalist would recognize as the *ecoregion* of the Northeast hardwoods, characterized by birch and beech in addition to conifers, with largely podzol and blue podzolic soils, and an annual rainfall of forty-five to forty-seven inches, highest in July and lowest in January. Within this broad language group were more than a dozen tribes, which settled and for centuries maintained separate and successful homelands in areas roughly coincident with what we could recognize as *georegions*. The Pennacook, for example, lived along the Merrimack River watershed, the Massachuset around Massachusetts Bay, the Montauk confederacy throughout most of Long Island, the Mahican along an extended Hudson River watershed from Lake Champlain down to the Catskills. And the pattern continues. Subtribes or language subgroups were distributed in areas roughly similar to *morphoregions*, smaller territories still matching geographical forms. In the Narragansett Bay georegion, the Wampanoag on the eastern shores and along the Sakonnet mouth were an ocean-directed people, while their cousins the Narragansets in the rest of the estuary, on up to the Blackstone, were riverine, and this distinctiveness was maintained by the distinctive lands on which the two groups depended for their livelihoods.

These Eastern Algonkian people, it seems, knew the land in much the same way that the modern ecologist knows it—or, rather, reports it—and as true dwellers in the land were early and unconscious bioregionalists.

There is further confirmation of American Indian habitation in bioregional patterns in the official treaty settlements signed by the US government with tribal leaders in the 19th and early 20th centuries. On a map of the areas established by these treaties—which were repeatedly and shamefully broken, but that's another story—it is easy to see, even in their imperfect form, the territories the original tribes once claimed as their homelands, and how to a remarkable degree they coincide with the various continental bioregions. On the Great Plains, for example, the treaty lines of the Kansa Indians follow to a large extent the Kansas River watershed; the Pawnee seem to have kept to the short-grass prairie bioregion along the Platte; the Osage were roughly coterminous with the Ozark Plateau; and so on.

Nothing demonstrates better how well grounded bioregionalism is than this kind of accordance, I think; nothing shows better how, far from being either an esoteric or exotic idea, or some made-up contrivance of contemporary do-gooders, it is a concept inherent in the cultures of age-old peoples who knew the ways of nature best. That is why I think the final distinctions about bioregional boundaries and the various scales at which to create human institutions can be safely left to people who live there, providing only that they have undertaken the job of honing their bioregional sensibilities and making acute their bioregional consciousnesses. It will be for them to learn and explore their surroundings, to draw and if necessary to redraw and redefine their comfortable territorial limits, and to readjust their organizations and settlements to match.

. . .

Here we come to the obvious second law of Gaea with regard to scale, and that has to do with the smaller sets of living webs, the natural human settlements within regions: communities. All biotic life is divided into communities, differing in size, complexity, development, and stability, but existing everywhere, throughout every econiche. If one were to look for the single basic building block of the ecological world, it would be the community.

For the ecologist, a community is an essentially self-sufficient and self-perpetuating collection of different species that have adapted as a whole to the conditions of their habitat. There may be only a comparatively few species, as in barren arctic regions where simple microorganisms predominate, or there may be thousands, as in a warm temperate forest where in a single acre (according to one estimate) there may be something like 50,000 vertebrates, 662,000 ants, 372,000 spiders, 90,000 earthworms, 45,000 termites, 19,000 snails, 89 million mites, 28 million collembola, and some 5,000 pounds of plant life divided into at least 2,000 species.

There are no exact limits on the geographical extent or number of organisms or total population of a biotic community, but there are general constraints that inevitably affect its structure and size. They have to do, more than anything else, with energy in its broadest sense: there are producers of energy (plants), consumers (from fungi to carnivores), and decomposers (from microorganisms to termites), and there must be some sort of circular balance among all of them for the successful life of the system. And when one or another species uses an unusual amount, the change will eventually affect all the other species and may in time lead to a new configuration of the community. For example, when tall shade plants begin to dominate a grove, using extra energy from sun and soils, they squeeze out certain other mid-sized species no longer able to get sufficient photosynthetic energy, but at the same time they allow many other shade-tolerant species to take root and thrive beneath them. Limits are established, too, by regional characteristics of climate and nutrients, the necessities that any species adapts to. Freshwater fish will not breed below the line where the highwater tide carries its salt, and grizzlies keep to the heaviest part of the wood where small game and fish are abundant.

The community, the bounded community, is not merely an abstract elaboration concocted by biologists or imposed by ecologists. It is the observable reality of a place, as real as the functions—as I see it in the summer outside my window—of the bumblebees pollinating the zucchini, the termites eating away the dead logs, the frogs in the stream catching insects, and the copperheads catching frogs. The animals and plants of course aren't conscious of being part of a niche of related organisms and don't sit around figuring out ways to adjust their communal harmony now that summer's here, or if the zucchini aren't blossoming. But their interaction, their connectedness, their communal interdependence is nonetheless as real as if it were indelibly codified and enforced. It is after all *how they live*, no more, no less.

Humans, too, live by community and always have, both that community joined to the surrounding species with which they interact for the necessities of life, and the purely human community with which they have evolved their unique social forms. Of the more than 100 billion people who have lived since the time of the Cro-Magnons, microbiologist René Dubos has noted, "the immense majority of them have spent their entire life as members of very small groups . . . rarely of more than a few hundred persons. The genetic determinants of behavior, and especially of social relationships, have thus evolved in small groups during several thousand generations." Nor, despite appearances in some places, has the community vanished even now. The eminent anthropologist George Peter Murdoch reported after an exhaustive ten-year cross-cultural survey that the institution of the community occurs "in every known human society," and there is no part of the world where people live alone or in isolated families: "Everywhere territorial propinquity, supported by divers other bonds, unites at least a few neighboring families into a larger social group."

As to the scale of the human community, there is a considerable body of information. I have gone into this in some detail elsewhere, so suffice it to say here that the human animal throughout its history—regardless of continent, climate, culture, or character—seems to have favored clusters of 500 to 1,000 people for the basic village or intimate settlement and 5,000 to 10,000 for the larger tribal association or extended community. Only rarely did agglomerations ever exceed this size, as with the capital cities of various empires, and even then they typically lasted for less than a century before shrinking to smaller sizes, as if there was some process at work making large cities inherently unstable and unsustainable, favoring those smaller human-scale settlements more suited to the limited capacity of human abilities.

The giant city, we must not forget, is a fairly recent enterprise of *Homo industrialus* (the first city to reach a million was London in the 1820s), and it has been sustained this long only at enormous social and political as well as sheer monetary cost, and through extremely complicated and ever more precarious support systems. It may prove in the long run to be simply an uncontinuable experiment, a violation of the laws of human and biotic nature that cannot be safely maintained, at least not on the scale we know today.

Certainly there is no question that the city of a million people, or even half a million most probably, has gone beyond the ecological balance point at which it is able to sustain itself on its own resources. Cities, particularly modern industrial cities, are like colonizers, grand suction systems drawing their life from everywhere in the surrounding nation, indeed the surrounding world, long since having gone past the point of adjusting to the carrying capacity of either their own territory or the nearby region's. A city of 1 million, it has been calculated, takes in 9,500 tons of fossil fuels, 2,000 tons of food, 625,000 tons of water, and 31,500 tons of oxygen *every day*—and puts out 500,000 tons of sewage, 28,500 tons of carbon dioxide, and great quantities of other solid, liquid, and gaseous wastes. The contemporary high-rise city, in short, is an ecological parasite as it extracts its lifeblood from elsewhere and an ecological pathogen as it sends back its wastes.

By contrast, the small community has historically been the most efficient at using energy, recycling its wastes, reducing drawdown, and adjusting to carrying capacity. A kind of unconscious wisdom operates at that level, I would argue, that is not necessarily available at other scales: the sensors of the society are most receptive, the feedback systems and information loops most effective, the decision-making mechanisms most adaptive and competent. This is the level, too, at which people have been shown to solve social problems most harmoniously, to survive randomness and change most easily, to know the maximum number of other people with some intimacy, and to retain a sense of the self-amid-others most salubriously. It is not by accident or divine decree, after all, that the limited community has lasted all these many millennia. It is because it was *experientially* the most effective form for survival.

· · ·

The bioregional mosaic, then, would seem logically to be made up basically of communities, as textured, developed, and complex as we could imagine, each having its own identity and spirit, but each of course having something in common with its neighbors in a shared bioregion. Even though the ultimate mosaic configuration would be bioregional, whether ecoregional, georegional, or morphoregional, its strength, its coherence, its color, and its luminosity would come from the various communitarian tesserae.

Something of the ultimate nature of this mosaic is suggested by the vision that was put forth over a decade ago by the authors of the British document that subsequently became a worldwide best-seller, *A Blueprint for Survival*:

> Although we believe that the small community should be the basic unit of society and that each community should be as self-sufficient and self-regarding as possible, we would like to stress that we are not proposing that they be inward-looking, self-obsessed or in any way closed to the rest of the world. Basic precepts of ecology, such as the interrelatedness of all things and the far-reaching effects of ecological processes and their disruption, should influence community decision-making, and therefore there must be an efficient and sensitive communications network between all communities.

Such a network, operating at one or more bioregional levels, would in fact be a neat enlargement of the other sorts of networks around us daily—the hills of ants, the hives of bees, the schools of fish, the flocks of birds—and join us in just the sort of enterprise Gaea has particularly suited us for: the gathering, sorting, processing, storing, and using of information.

SIX

Economy

EDWARD GOLDSMITH, the iconoclastic Englishman who is editor of the sharp and scholarly British magazine *The Ecologist*, a few years ago proposed two laws of "ecodynamics" that he wished to set up against the more familiar laws of thermodynamics. The trouble with the thermodynamic postulates, he argued, was that they were drawn from and applied essentially to *closed* systems such as steam engines and were grossly misleading when applied to an *open* system such as the biosphere. Living systems in "the real world," he indicated, do not show any particular signs of the famous entropy laws, by which energy is held to be continually dissipated and transformed and complex systems held to be continually simplified and disorderly. Indeed, the living biosphere constantly receives new energy from the outside (heat from the sun, gravitational energy from the moon, radiation from the cosmos, etc.), and it shows every indication, over the long eons of time, of becoming essentially more complex and more diverse:

Life probably began on this planet three thousand million years ago and since then—that is until the beginning of the historical era a mere ten thousand years ago—it has not ceased to develop both in complexity, diversity and stability . . . *in a manner that is diametrically opposed to that in which it should have behaved had it been governed by the Entropy Law.*

The laws of the real world, Goldsmith suggests, might best be put this way:

1. The First Law of Ecodynamics:

Conservation is the basic goal of behaviour. . . . But it is not just matter that behaviour seeks to conserve or preserve but *structure.* . . . The adaptive response to radical environmental changes is to *oppose* them and reverse them rather than to accommodate them. . . . Living things seek to conserve their information, structure and behaviour.

2. The Second Law of Ecodynamics: "Natural systems tend towards stability," not in the direction of "entropy" or disorder but toward climax:

Once a climax is achieved then they cease to grow. . . . Any growth over and above the climax state cannot be progress in ecological terms since it will be achievable by violating basic biospheric laws—which must lead to biospheric disintegration, hence a diversion from the optimum organisation. . . . Climax must correspond to ecological equilibrium.*

If the economy that comes into being in a bioregion is to begin anywhere, it would logically be right there: a bioregional economy would seek *first* to maintain rather than use

---

*This climax state, it should be emphasized, is not normally static and unchanging, for over years and decades both gradual natural processes and sudden natural disruptions may force changes in and readjustments of species. But it is always the mature state to which the ecosystem tends, wherein such alterations are best accommodated and long-term dislocations minimized.

up the natural world, to adapt to the environment rather than try to exploit or manipulate it, to *conserve* not only the resources but also the relationships and systems of the natural world; and *second* to establish a *stable* means of production and exchange rather than one always in flux and dependent upon continual growth and constant consumption, in service to something called "progress," a false and delusory goddess if ever there was one. An economy, in other words, that would not be a different thing from the ecology, as it is today—they both stem after all from the same Greek root, *oikos*, for household—but would be meshed and linked with it, thoroughly compatible with it.

So, at its base, it would be an economy that depended upon a *minimum* number of goods and the *minimum* amount of environmental disruption along with the *maximum* use of renewable resources and the *maximum* use of human labor and ingenuity. For energy, it would obviously depend on the various forms of solar power appropriate to the region; for transportation, on human-powered machines and electric vehicles and trains, along with settlement patterns that encourage walking and biking; for agriculture, on organic and pest-management farming, perennial polyculture, aquaculture, and permaculture, with markets geared to seasonal and regional foods supplemented by extensive greenhouse use; for industry, on local crafters and artisans rather than factory production, on natural materials and nonpolluting processes, emphasizing durability and quality. And so on: at all points, in all processes, a system whose goals would be to cut down on energy and resource use, minimize production and "throughput," reward conservation and recycling, and hold population and commodity stocks at a roughly constant and balanced level. *Growth* would not be its goal, but *sustainability*.

Such an economy, in spite of its distance from the present

69

one, is really not all that difficult to imagine, and indeed many of its workings have been written about quite extensively in recent years by those scholars who have advocated a system of "soft-energy paths" and "conservancy" and "eco-consciousness"—or what has generally come to be called the "steady-state" economy. Not that these scholars are necessarily bioregionalists, of course, but they have been led along their own separate byways to an understanding of how important an ecological sensibility is in refashioning an economy of permanence and stability. One of the earliest and most insightful of them, Herman E. Daly, professor of economics at Louisiana State University, speaks of the connection this way:

> A steady-state economy fits easily into the paradigm of physical science and biology—the earth approximates a steady-state open system, as do organisms. Why not our economy also, at least in its physical dimensions of bodies and artifacts? Economists forgot about physical dimensions long ago and centered their attention on value. But the fact that wealth is measured in value units does not annihilate its physical dimensions. Economists may continue to maximize value, and value could conceivably grow forever, but the physical mass in which value inheres must conform to a steady state, and the constraints of physical constancy on value growth will be severe and must be respected.

Even economists, in sum, when they go home at night, must live in the real, abiding, physical world.

And there, late at night, after their econometric analyses and labor theories have been put away, they might reflect on these physical limitations, the Gaean reality, and ask themselves: if economics is the science of the distribution and use of the earth's resources, every single one of which without exception is derived from a finite ecosphere, why has it come up with nothing but systems that will use those resources all up?

. . .

I can understand that there may be residual fears that a bioregional economy based on stability and conservation would mean terrible deprivation, a loss of all our material gains, a reversion to some kind of hand-to-mouth existence where we'd all be living in caves and plucking berries. I will leave the complex refutation of that to others specifically qualified, among them such distinguished steady-state economists as Kenneth Boulding, E. J. Mishan, Nicholas Georgescu-Roegen, and E. F. Schumacher—the full list of works may be found at the end of this book, and I can assure you that they have established the position beyond the cavil of all but the most willfully blind—but it might be worthwhile to examine briefly the inevitable question of "standards of living" and what the bioregional future would hold.

Let's start from this premise: since it's fairly obvious that we cannot go on much longer measuring standards of living by the traditional methods of reckless drawdown and heedless growth, we will have to start thinking in other terms. We will have to measure our lives in terms of clean air rather than large cars, of healthy chemical-free food rather than supermarket frozen convenience, of autonomous workplaces rather than fat paychecks, of days without rush hours and TV commercials and junk mail. Such things are not measurable by the traditional GNP (aptly called *gross*) but they are not without value—indeed for many they are of primary value—and in any sensible reckoning ought to be considered part of one's living standard. The bioregional economy must be labor-intensive rather than energy-intensive, so it will provide more jobs. It must produce more durable goods in order to reduce waste, so it will emphasize quality rather than quantity. It must reduce pollution of air, water, and food, so it will improve public health. It must eliminate the inflation inherent in a growth economy, so it will make income, expenditures, and whole currencies more stable. There are values there, I think evident to anyone, more values in the bioregional system, Horatio, than are dreamt of in the usual economic accounting.

Moreover, it would be madness, all other things aside, to scorn a future economic system simply because it fails to live up to a present one that is both grossly inequitable and highly unstable. I don't for a moment deny that the last century of drawdown has produced an enormous and extravagant instance of what ecologists call *bloom*—a period of unusually rapid growth when ecosystems spread out quickly and use great quantities of energy to support first-stage consumers—and the United States has created one of the most prosperous material societies in the world. But we've done it, as almost all scholars acknowledge, by an excessive, exploitative, unusual, and uncontinuable use of the world's resources—something on the order of 30 to 40 percent of them nowadays, to support a mere 6 percent of the world's population.

Even then, in spite of its clear trickle-down effects for some, it is not the sort of bloom that has benefited all that much of the population. There are, by official and officially slippery figures, something between 35 and 50 million Americans living in serious poverty and facing actual hunger; the richest one-fifth of American families have over 40 percent of the national income (41 percent in 1980) and have had for decades; only half of all families have a net worth of even $4,000; and the top 5 percent own fully half the nation's wealth, whereas the bottom 25 percent actually own nothing or indeed are in debt.

A bloom of extravagance and inequity: that's not something so precious to cling to, it seems to me, so necessarily unalterable, something so obviously neat and effective that it makes rational alternatives unworthy of consideration.

Especially when one of those alternatives offers so much else.

· · ·

One further precept follows from the two laws of ecodynamics, a precept as inherent in the ecosphere as oxygen, the most elemental and elegant principle of the natural world: self-sufficiency. It is the way the biosphere and all its ecosystems go about the central task of *achieving* conservation and stability and hence why all the long-established homeostatic, and evolutionary, processes of nature work toward self-regulation, self-reliance, self-empowerment.

Let us take a healthy mature ecosystem. The sources of energy are immediate and renewable, the level of resource use is sustainable, wastes and detritus are returned to the earth without environmental damage. The various species, linked together and to the environment in a necessary if unconscious dependency, adapt quickly and at many different levels to changing circumstances. Outside or asystemic agents are normally detected and rejected, so the total population is stable, and within the system population levels of the species are maintained in a dynamic equilibrium. The system also resists forces from inside or outside, even theoretically benevolent ones, that try to extend the ecosystem beyond its borders or induce it to grow beyond its limits. This is a mature and stable system of self-sufficiency.

It is interesting, and probably not accidental, that in many respects such a description can be applied to most tribal or preliterate societies as well. Successful early societies were of course self-sufficient by necessity—almost by definition, because if they weren't, they simply wouldn't have existed—and developed over long ages systems with just that same kind of self-reliant use of the environment, the same self-regulating adaptiveness, the same self-regarding independence, the same self-limiting sustainability.

In the natural realm self-sufficiency is not normally found at the level of one species or small community, because there interdependency is the rule: the beehive, however self-contained and self-regulated it may be, absolutely depends upon nearby trees and flowers and natural materials for its existence. But at the level of the ecosystem, self-sufficiency is the norm, for at that level there is a sufficiently abundant population for successful interaction among the species and a sufficiently wide territory for resources to sustain them all.

The same rule seems appropriate for human self-sufficiency as well. It is no doubt possible for a community of a thousand people to carve out a living for itself, dependent on a wide range of plant and animal species but totally isolated from other human communities; but then it is also possible for a single individual to live a hermetic life of perpetual isolation deep in the backwoods that would have to be called self-sufficient. For a fully enriched and developed life, however, for the possibilities not only of material enrichment and convivial association but also cultural enlargement, surely a wider circle than that is desirable. And for anything approaching the standard where we might have a wide range of food, some choice in necessities and some sophistication in luxuries, the population to sustain a university and a large hospital and a

symphony orchestra, a full-scale morphoregion would seem
to be necessary.

Within almost any imaginable bioregion in North America
or elsewhere (with significant exceptions in certain brutally
ravaged parts of Africa and Asia), there are sufficient resources
to provide a stable and satisfying life, though indeed their
abundance and splendor might vary greatly. Certainly there
is not a single bioregion in this country, even at the georegional
level, that would not, if it looked to all its natural endowments,
be able to provide its residents with sufficient food,
energy, shelter, and clothing, their own health care and education
and arts, their own manufactures and crafts. Each region
would need to learn to adapt to its natural circumstances,
developing energy based on available resources (wind in the
Rockies, water in New England, wood in the Northwest),
growing food appropriate to the climate and soils, creating
crafts and industries according to the given ores and minerals,
woods and leathers, cloths and yarns. And where this or that
material or mineral may be missing, and not to be found for
recycling in regional dumps and fills, each bioregion would
have to depend primarily upon that human inspiration that
always rises to the surface in time of need and opportunity—
as, for example, the US government learned to derive rubber
from the once-ignored guayule plant of the Southwestern
desert during World War II, when rubber supplies from
abroad were threatened. Necessity being the mother of invention,
we may safely call self-sufficiency the grandmother.

Adjustments there would have to be, to be sure, and some
bioregions would have to steel themselves for significant
changes from their omniverous and gluttonous habits of the
present: noncitrus regions would need to look to other sources
of vitamin C, for example, cattle-herding regions to diversify

into fruits and vegetables, lumber-importing regions to turn to adobe or brick, plastic-importing regions to glass (sand is available everywhere on this continent) or local wood and rubber substitutes. Substitutability, in fact, is a great deal easier than is usually assumed, and in recent years a considerable amount of scholarly attention has been devoted to it, obviously with particular regard to those metals that are both valuable and essentially nonrenewable such as mercury, copper, nickel, zinc, cadmium, and tin. And where substitutions are not immediately practical, a careful recycling of the existing elements can keep them in sufficient supply for a very long time to come; significant amounts of lead, iron, copper, nickel, antimony, mercury, and aluminum are already being recycled from scrap in this country through well-established processes, and much more could be done where the need was evident.

. . .

These kinds of adjustments need not be sudden, or hard, or privative, and they could be planned with great care and sophistication once the bioregional stocks and supplies are fully known. Far from being deprived, far from being thus impoverished, even the most unendowed bioregion can in the long run *gain* in economic health with a careful and deliberate policy of self-sufficiency. The reasons are various:

1. A self-sufficient bioregion would be more economically stable, more in control of investment, production, and sales, and hence more insulated from the cycles of boom-and-bust engendered by distant market forces or remote political crises. And its people, with a full close-up knowledge of both markets and resources, would be able to allocate their products and labor in the most efficient way, to build and develop what and where they want to at the safest pace, to control their own

money supply and currency value without extreme fluctuations—*and* to adjust all those procedures with comparative ease when necessary.

2. A self-sufficient bioregion would not be in vassalage to far-off and uncontrollable national bureaucracies or transnational corporations, at the mercy of whims or greeds of politicians and plutocrats. Not caught up in the vortex of worldwide trade, it would be free from the vulnerability that *always* accompanies dependence in some degree or other, as the Western world discovered with considerable pain when OPEC countries quadrupled the price of the oil it depended on, as the non-Western world experiences daily.

3. A self-sufficient bioregion would be, plainly put, richer than one enmeshed in extensive trade, even when the trade balance is favorable. Partly this is because no part of the economy need be devoted to paying for imports, a burden that severely taxes even an industrial country like the United States—where, try as we might, we have not escaped a severe trade deficit in the last fifteen years—and that simply drains nations heavily dependent on imports, such as Britain, Brazil, Mexico, and most of the nonindustrial Third World. Partly this is because enterprises can devote themselves to their own markets and undertake what Jane Jacobs calls "import-replacement," a process with economic and creative multiplier effects that enrich all segments of the economy. And partly this is because the region does not have to spend its money on one of the all-important costs of any commodity—in many cases the predominant cost—of transportation.

4. A self-sufficient bioregion would be in control of its own currency, so it could receive immediate feedback on the workings of the economy and avoid the structural flaws that beset

most regions whose money is largely controlled from without. Local currencies, moreover, can be kept steady and basically free from inflation (especially if hoarding is discouraged by taxing accumulation), can be manipulated to bolster faltering industries or services, and can usually be confined to the region to encourage reinvestment and prevent the flight of capital.

5. A self-sufficient bioregion, finally, would be healthier and able to enjoy a more productive economy on the one hand while escaping the massive expenditures of medical treatment on the other. Not only could it be free of the chronic diseases of industrialization—cancer, ischemic heart disease, diabetes, diverticulitis, tooth caries—that are known to increase in perfect synchronization with the GNP, but it can spare itself the applied toxicity we now take for granted. Locally grown and marketed foods, for example, do not need to be sprayed with chemicals to make them appealing or increase their shelf-life, nor to be stored with insecticides and rodenticides, nor to be processed and packaged with polymers and plastics. Besides, being fresher, they will simply be more nutritious.

There is one last and obvious benefit to self-sufficiency, though I hesitate to list it on a strictly economic ledger despite the clear advantages it brings to any sane economy. It is that it fosters of necessity a more cohesive, more self-regarding, more self-concerned populace, with a developed sense of community and comradeship as well as the pride and resiliency that come with the knowledge of one's competence, control, stability, and independence. "Reverse cannot befall that fine Prosperity," wrote Emily Dickinson, "whose sources are interior."

· · ·

Self-sufficiency, I must add before I am badly misunderstood, is not the same thing as isolation, nor does it preclude all kinds of trade at all times. It does not *require* connections with the outside, but within strict limits—the connections must be nondependent, nonmonetary, and noninjurious—it allows them. And, in one area, it encourages them.

There are no barriers to knowledge, and it would be foolish to imagine constructing them. Indeed, it may be the self-sufficient society that most needs information from without—about new techniques and inventions, new materials and designs, and innovations scientific, cultural, technical, political, and otherwise. The society secure in its competence and satisfied in its needs would do best to keep itself open to ideas from beyond its edges, its antennae ever alert.

But the flow of ideas possible in a bioregional world would be quite different from the sort that is regularized today. All that speaks of the global, or monocultural, or hemispheric would be really irrelevant to any self-regarding bioregion; what it would want would be information and experience specific to the kind of environment it inhabited. This is not likely to come from the bioregion next door, which would have different characteristics, and it may not even come from any other bioregion on that continent. But there are bound to be any number of places somewhere else in the world that have enough of the same ecological conditions to be ideal partners with which to share ideas; and there are likely to be so many of them in a diverse and self-sufficient world that all kinds of pertinent experiments would have been tried and a wealth of information garnered.

An interesting example of just such a bioregional interchange exists even in this era. A bioregional group in Austin, Texas, called the Center for Maximum Potential Building Systems—known more familiarly as Max's Pot—was recently trying to figure out some use for the mesquite trees growing so freely in the savanna of the Colorado River bioregion surrounding Austin that they are regularly eradicated as a weed. The Max's Pot people knew that mesquite wood was extremely hard, twice as hard as hickory and oak and with a density close to ebony, but they were stumped by the fact that the trees grow like spindly shrubs, with none of the long straight trunks and limbs from which marketable lumber normally comes.

Being a bioregional pioneer, the founder of Max's Pot, Pliny Fisk III, decided to find out if there were other regions where mesquite grew and what the people there did with mesquite wood. "Our search," Fisk relates, "led us to two sister bioregions: the Argentinian and Uruguayan pampas."

> In these bioregions, mesquite is extensively used as parquet floor tile. Many of the manufacturing facilities necessary for making these wood tiles are relatively small-scale, staffed by five to seven employees. Yet, even with seemingly small productive capacity, the quantity of the mesquite parquet floor tile actually produced in parts of Argentina is approximately equivalent to the amount of carpet used in our own bioregion. Our center is presently studying the technology and economics of scale that our biome neighbors have discovered to see whether or not this technology could have use with our own people. At the same time, we see ourselves as sharing techniques we have developed which use the mesquite sawdust to make into an insulating building block, as well as how portable charcoal kilns can be used to make mesquite scrap material into a high-BTU, clean-burning fuel.

Self-sufficiency, or in this case the contemplation of it, can lead to productive exchanges far beyond the bioregion itself, not entangling or compromising but actually reinforcing self-reliance.

. . .

And thus we come, organically almost, to the final precept hinging on the two laws of ecodynamics: the principle of cooperation.

As natural systems tend toward conservation and stability by the workings of self-regulation, the Gaean premium is obviously upon the associations that create harmony rather than discord, equilibrium rather than turbulence. The successful ecosystem requires its many parts to operate smoothly together, regularized and dependent over time. As *The Ecologist's* Edward Goldsmith puts it:

> They must co-operate with each other and behave in that way that will satisfy the requirements of the system of which they are a part, and hence contribute to the latter's stability or survival. This they do . . . because they have been designed phylogenetically and ontogenetically to fulfill the requisite differentiated functions. It is by fulfilling them, in fact, that their relationship with the various constituents of their environment is the most stable—that they are thereby best adjusted to their environment.

There's no question about cooperation being the underlying principle of nonhuman life forms. Lynn Margulis's work, for one, shows conclusively that stromatolitic bacteria—about the most ancient form of life that we have been able to discover—have structures and functions quite similar to those found in all higher plants and animals, arguing that lifeforms over these countless millennia have been based on "an interlinking, highly cooperating, and organized set of bacterial components." There's also not very much question about cooperation having been the underlying principle of all early human societies. The killer-ape human of pseudo-anthropology once popular in the West has been discredited now, and the theories of people like the Leakeys in Kenya and C. K. Brain and Elizabeth Vrba have pretty well established that a basic sense of mutual aid was instrumental in the success of hominid communities as early as 3.5 million years ago.

In fact, the Darwinian notion that evolution favored the survival of the fittest individual through ceaseless competition has by now generally given way to the understanding that evolutionary success was due to the survival of the fittest *community* through interlocking cooperation. Those families and bands that united and learned to cooperate for the tending of fire, the sharing of food, the hunting of large animals, the securing of campsites (or in current anthropological parlance, "home bases"), were more likely to survive than any others. That kind of cooperation, then, over several *hundred thousand* years, actually inbred in the human species—Dubos and other biologists argue that it is genetically encoded—the qualities of collaboration, teamwork, sodality, and federation.

The lesson for the bioregional economy is obvious enough: the marketplace of our traditional capitalist economy, with its emphasis on competition, exploitation, and individual profit, needs to be phased out. E. F. Schumacher, a professional economist and for twenty years the chief economist of Britain's National Coal Board, came to see this clearly enough: "The market represents only the surface of society," he wrote, "and its significance relates to the momentary situation as it exists there and then. There is no probing into the depths of things, into the natural or social facts that lie behind them." It simply does not reflect the real—the ecological—world.

"It is inherent in the methodology of economics to ignore man's dependence on the natural world," Schumacher pointed out, and this is why the market makes no distinctions at all between *primary* goods, "which man has to win from nature," and *secondary* goods, which are all the things manufactured from them. This is why the market does not distinguish between renewable and nonrenewable resources, and in fact tends to value more highly those that are certain to run out (e.g., petroleum) and especially those that are already quite scarce (e.g., gold). And this is why the market ignores the whole idea of social or environmental costs, setting prices on an object that reflect only the actual expenses (plus profits) of the sellers and take no account of whatever damage may have been done to the earth in extraction, whatever pollution may have been created in manufacture, whatever toll may have been put on the infrastructure in distribution, whatever expenses may be involved in disposal, and so on and on. It is an industrio-scientific marketplace, not a Gaean one.

The notion of a cooperative rather than a competitive economy is so at odds with the Western experience of the last 500 years that imagining what it would look like is indeed difficult. But we should remember that what we take for granted in our market system—what we assume to be the "human nature" of buyers and sellers—is really a rather recent development. In the simple economies of most societies before the modern age, in the tribal and peasant economies known to anthropologists, there is an entirely different set of assumptions and values at work, most often aiming at social harmony rather than personal gain. As the scholars reconstruct them—I'm thinking of Marshall Sahlins's *Stone Age Economy* and Karl Polanyi's *The Great Transformation* among others—they seem to have much that a bioregional society could learn from: goods valued for their utility or beauty rather than cost; commodities exchanged more on the basis of need than of exchange value; distribution to the society at large without regard to labor that members have invested; labor performed without the idea of a wage return or individual benefit, indeed largely without the notion of "work" at all. (A great many early societies simply had no word for "work," the idea being foreign to cultures where no activity is undertaken that is not a custom or a ritual or a spontaneous part of social congress, and where seldom does anyone have to be forced or coaxed to perform it.)

. . .

Suppose that strange sort of communal model were adopted by a bioregional society: what would be the tenets of it in contemporary terms?

To begin with, presumably, there would be a sense that the wealth of nature is the wealth of all—people should not be able to *own* the land, or its ores, or its trees, any more than they can own the sky and its clouds—and whatever is taken from Gaea's realm is not to be hoarded and used for personal glory but distributed and used for regional benefit. Bioregional economies would thus be designed for sharing: a population of such-and-such a size, we can figure, needs x many acres planted with y many crops, a certain predictable amount of annual energy, so many tons of this and pounds of that resource, a calculable gallonage of drinkable water, and so on, and the job of the economy is to produce just the right amount so that in normal conditions each individual and family and community can have its fair share. If there is production over and above this calculable amount, some can be stored for future lean years, some exchanged in the marketplace, some turned into methane or fountains or fireworks or sculptures. Insofar as complicated exchanges of goods and services are necessary, money as the medium could be serviceable—though it is well to remember that more societies in history have operated on barter and potlatch and communality than ever have done on money—so long as it is based on local resources and local conditions, controlled by local institutions. *Ownership*—of field and factory, store and studio, workshop and warehouse, all units beyond the obviously private— might logically be in community rather than regional or individual hands, but a long history of self-interest suggests that individuals and families might be given rights to the *use*, or usufruct, of goods and lands for their own benefit.

What helps to remove all that kind of speculation from the realm of fantasy, as unfamiliar as it may at first look, is that many components of this sort of economy have already been worked out, have already been tried and tested in the hugger-mugger of the real world—and the contemporary one at that. To take just two examples:

Communal ownership. In contemporary America the most fruitful example of communal ownership—though there are in truth many examples, from building co-ops in major cities to communes in the hinterlands—is the community land trust. The CLT is a nonprofit corporation, open to all members of a local community, that acquires a parcel of land to be held in trust in perpetuity and then rents it out on long-term, low-cost leases, renewable and inheritable, restricted by whatever original agreements the trust makes as to ecological practices, kinds of building, pooling of surplusses, and the like. It is very simple and very practical, which is one reason the movement has grown so rapidly in the decade and a half since its inception, with more than fifty CLTs now operating in the US. It stands as concrete evidence that not even Americans need to *own* their land individually to care about it, to work it, and to build on it, knowing that the fruits of their labor ultimately go not only to their own posterity but to the posterity of the larger community as well.

Local economies. Community-based currencies were quite common in the early years of the American colonies, whether informal—chits and "duebills" exchanged at the general store, or formal—tobacco (and tobacco "warehouse receipts") as legal tender in Virginia from 1642 on. In times of crisis community money and trading systems have popped up in many places, most notably in Germany and Austria during the 1930s and in Chicago in the late Depression. In current times such schemes have taken a wide variety of forms, from labor and trade exchanges to barter systems to local currencies based on world-traded commodities. In British Columbia, for example, a wide circle of people uses a computer-based system of local "script" money in conjunction with official currency; Amish and Mennonite communities in Pennsylvania and New York operate as far as possible outside the national economy with various forms of barter, chits, and communal agreements as the media of exchange among themselves; and the town of Winona, Minnesota, for several years has run a barter and credit-note system called the Free Trade Exchange, in which local citizens trade services and goods—baby-sitting, typing, firewood, food—through a collective pool, entirely removed from the national economy. And in Great Barrington, Massachusetts, the E. F. Schumacher Society has fostered a plan to issue a true local currency based on and backed by local cordwood—a widely available, renewable, and labor-intensive resource—to be used and deposited only in the Berkshire bioregion. The possibilities are manifold—and manifest.

• • •

A few years ago two regional planners at UCLA put out a typically academic book called *Territory and Function: The*

Evolution of Regional Planning, in the middle of which was a remarkable and fascinating section devoted to what they called the "agropolitan" region. As envisioned by John Friedmann and Clyde Weaver, such a region would be a careful blend of country and city, agriculture and industry, operating as a self-governing unit and controlling its own finances and economy. As professionals, they proposed this scheme as the basis for future development not only in developing countries but in industrial ones as well. Obviously they were, quite unknowingly, squarely in the bioregional tradition.

Their comments on an "agropolitan" economy are necessarily speculative, but they are based on a good deal of experience around the world and are certainly suggestive in bioregional terms:

> Agropolitan development builds strength from within, based on its own resources, its own skills, its own discoveries and learning. It does not expect a transfusion of strength from "donor" countries abroad. It does not count on miraculous transformations, nor on results without effort. And so it begins with a development that will satisfy basic needs as, in doing so, it creates new ones.
>
> If the countryside is endowed with basic infrastructure—for instance, if an internal communications and transport network is built up that will connect agropolitan districts and regions with each other—large cities will lose their present overwhelming advantage. The economy will then turn inward upon itself, discover its hidden energies and assets, and, in a "natural" learning progression, modernize itself from within.
>
> Manufacturing industry will be second in a logical sequence of steps. The first is the continuous upgrading of agricultural productions, starting with overall increases in the physical volume of food and basic fibres, followed, in due course, by increases in the productivity of farm land and the productivity of workers.
>
> The development of industry will be tied into this sequence,

beginning with agricultural processing and going on to the manufacture of tools and other equipment of use to peasants and workers in their daily lives. Dispersed among the villages and fields, small industries will provide a source of work and income, in a mode of production that is intimately related to the emerging agropolitan structure of society in which the contradictions of industrial capitalism—between city and countryside, production and consumption, work and lei-sure—are progressively resolved.

Now all that may sound slightly utopian, slightly wide-eyed. But these are experts, men concerned for many years with regions and how they can and should work. Besides, they stand firmly in the company of G. A. Borgese, a visionary credited with these wonderful words: "It is necessary; there-fore it is possible."

SEVEN

Polity

ONE OF THE FEW notable world religions to understand the primacy of the natural world in human spirituality—perhaps the only one at all widespread—is the Taoism of the Chinese sage and political philosopher Lao Tzu:

> The valley spirit never dies;
> It is the woman—Primal Mother;
> Her Gateway is the root of Heaven and Earth;
> Like a veil it is barely seen,
> But use it—it will never fail.

It is not surprising then, that this religion is one of the few to advocate the decentralization of political power, the values of village and communal life, and the goal of egalitarian rather than hierarchical status in familial and kinship relations. The famous admonition "Let things alone" was not merely a caution for humans to show a proper respect for the workings of nature but, in the context of the *Tao te Ching*, primarily advice for Chinese princes and warlords of the 6th century BC: the best government is not merely the least government, Lao Tzu seems to say, but no government at all.

We may assume that Lao Tzu came to his political wisdom

by way of his ecological insights, for his Taoism is infused with those substantial laws of Gaea that express themselves time and again in the natural world. A political vision based on those laws, on the evident workings of the biotic world, would not celebrate centralized coordination, hierarchical efficiency, and monolithic strength—the apparent virtues of the modern nation-state—but rather, in starkest contraposition, decentralization, interdependence, and diversity. The ways of nature, in any park, on any shore, in any woods, are essentially without coercion, without organized force, without recognized authority. They are, to pick the closest word in our inadequate vocabulary, *libertarian*.

It is perhaps inevitable that a civilization based on the denial of Gaean principles should evolve its forms of government so at odds with natural laws. But the experiment has been tried now for perhaps two hundred years (the duration of parliamentary and representative "democracies") or, in its modern version, for perhaps a hundred (the duration of the welfare state), and it is no longer startling to suggest that it may simply have failed. Certainly modern governments, capitalist or socialist, have not addressed themselves in any serious way to the relationship between the crisis of ecological peril and the political systems that have caused it. (Tame and meliorative air-pollution laws, for only one example, have nothing to do with true ecological wisdom or a thoroughgoing ecological policy.) They have not solved the problems of world overpopulation, or recurrent and growing epidemics of starvation, or accelerating economic inequality, or mounting social dislocation (crime, suicide, alcoholism, stress diseases, etc.). Maybe it is simply impossible for institutions insufficiently based in natural principles to understand and confront the profound complexities of a Gaean world; perhaps they stand no better chance of surviving within that world than the Mycenaeans.

Whatever dangers and uncertainties a bioregional polity may hold, then—however strange and impractical and otherworldly it may strike those for whom, say, the American government seems a rational and serviceable institution—it must be granted at least the virtue of ecological compatibility. If it should ever be given the chance to evolve into being, no matter what its other drawbacks, it would at a minimum have a chance to stop and reverse the ecocidal policies of the present, to readjust priorities away from human primacy and toward human interdependence, and to offer a reasonable possibility that the globe will continue to have complex life upon it after the 21st century. And if it should fail in that, however improbable it seems, it will not have done worse than the industrial polities it replaced.

. . .

The ecological law with which bioregional politics would logically begin is decentralism, centrifugal force, the spreading of power to small and widely dispersed units.

So it is in the natural world, where nothing is more striking than the absence of any centralized control, any interspeciate domination, where there are none of the patterns of ruler-and-ruled that are taken as inevitable in human governance. "King of the jungle" is *our* description of the lion's status, and quite anthropomorphously perverse; the lion (or, better, lioness) is profoundly unaware of this role, and the elephant and rhinoceros (not to mention the tsetse fly) would hardly accede to it. In a biotic community the various sets of animals and plants, no matter how they may run their own families and clusters, behave smoothly and regularly with each other without the need of any overall system of authority or dominance, any biotic Washington or Wall Street, in fact without any governing organization or superstructure of any kind soever. No one species rules over all—or any—others, not one even makes the attempt, not one even has either instinct or intention in that direction. (Even the kudzu and the red-tide bacteria, for all that they sometimes look as if they have in mind to conquer the world, are merely blindly moving into comfortable new environments and have no thought of rule or enslavement.)

What's more, when several subgroups of a single species occupy the same region, there is no attempt to consolidate power in one of them: you never see one colony of crows try to conquer another, one pride of lions try to establish control over all the other lions around. *Territoriality*, yes: often a subgroup of a species attempts to carve out a part of the eco-niche for itself and goes to considerable lengths to keep other members of that species (and competing species) away. But that is not governance, not the creation of any central author-ity, it is merely a familial or communal statement about the carrying capacity of that niche for that species—and, I guess, of who was there first to measure it. And *defense*, too: there can be quite intense and deadly conflict when one subgroup defends its home—hive or hill, roost or lair—from another, and mammalian families and individuals will often go to great lengths, including aggression at times, to protect females and their young during birth and nesting periods. But these are not battles of conquest, they are not followed by domination or colonization (though some ants will take other ants as pris-oners), and they are never caused by one subgroup desiring to establish its rule, its command, over another.

Now there is of course one continuous exercise of power between species in the ecosphere: many animals perforce de-pend on ingesting other animals and a wide range of plants. There is in fact a regular practice we call *predation* by which

92

certain species live in a quasi-symbiotic relationship of hunter
and hunted, eater and eaten, and it is common among all biotic
communities and among many species of animals as well as a
few plants. But this is not governance, it is not rule or dominance, it is not even aggression of an organized political or
military kind. Mosquitoes, whatever they may be said to
think, do not believe that they are *ruled over* by the purple
martin that plucks the unlucky ones out of the air; and zebras,
however wary they may always be at the watering hole, do
not regard themselves as being in an inferior position to the
lion or under the regular administration of some larger species. The predatory relationship is certainly one of violence
and death (and sustenance and life), certainly one of imbalance
and nonreciprocation, but it is never undertaken for anything
but food—not for governance, or control, or the establishment of power or sovereignty. An exercise of power it is, but
it is still diffused power, almost *accidental* power. (Moreover,
there is always some kind of mutuality at work in predation,
even though it is of an unconscious kind and may go quite
unappreciated by the predatee; one could not really expect the
caribou to welcome the attack by the gray wolf pack, though
in fact it is a necessary means of controlling the herd's population, and by weaning out the weakest and sickest helps to
strengthen the herd's genetic heritage.)

A similar kind of decentralism, a recurrent urge toward separatism, independence, and local autonomy rather than ag-
glomeration and concentration, exists in human patterns as
well. Throughout all human history, even in the past several
hundred years, people have tended to live in separate and independent small groups, a "fragmentation of human society"
that Harold Isaacs, the venerated professor of international
affairs at MIT, has described as something akin to "a pervasive

93

force in human affairs and always has been." Even when nations and empires have arisen, he notes, they have no staying power against the innate human drive toward decentralism:

> The record shows that there could be all kinds of lags, that declines could take a long time and falls run long overdue, but that these conditions could never be indefinitely maintained. Under external or internal pressures—usually both—authority was eroded, legitimacy challenged, and in wars, collapse, and revolution, the system of power redrawn.

And, as he surveys the cataclysms of the 20th century, Isaacs shows that the fragmenting process has operated everywhere in our time, breaking down empires, throwing off new nations, distending and dividing old ones, "a great clustering into separateness":

> What we are experiencing, then, is not the shaping of new coherences but the world breaking into its bits and pieces, bursting like big and little stars from exploding galaxies, each one spinning off in its own centrifugal whirl, each one straining to hold its own small separate pieces from spinning off in their turn.

The political lessons are clear enough, I think: a bioregional polity would seek the diffusion of power, the decentralization of institutions, with nothing done at a level higher than necessary, and all authority flowing upward incrementally from the smallest political unit to the largest.

The primary location of decision-making, therefore, and of political and economic control, should be the community, the more-or-less intimate grouping either at the close-knit village scale of 1,000 people or so, or probably more often at the extended community scale of 5,000 to 10,000 so often found as the fundamental political unit whether formal or informal. Here, where people know one another and the essentials of the environment they share, where at least the most basic information for problem-solving is known or readily available, here is where governance should begin. Decisions made at this level, as countless eons testify, stand at least a fair chance of being correct and a reasonable likelihood of being carried out competently; and even if the choice is misguided or the implementation faulty, the damage to either the society or the ecosphere is likely to be insignificant. This is the sort of government established by preliterate peoples all over the globe, evolving over the years toward a kind of bedrock efficiency in problem-solving simply because it is necessary for survival. In the tribal councils, the folkmotes, the ecclesia, the village assemblies, the town meetings, we find the human institution proven through time to have shown the scope and competence for the most basic kind of self-rule.

As different species live side by side in an ecosystem, so different communities could live side by side in a single city, and cities and towns side by side in a single bioregion, with no more thought of dominance and control than the sparrow gives to the rose, or the bobcat to the wasp. Sharing the same bioregion, they naturally share the same configurations of life, the same social and economic constraints, roughly the same environmental problems and opportunities, and so there is every reason to expect contact and cooperation among them. Even, for some specific tasks, maybe even confederation among them—but of a kind that need not mean diminished power or sovereignty for the community, but rather enlarged horizons of knowledge, of culture, of services, of security.

Of course communities with a bioregional consciousness would find countless occasions that called for regional cooperation—and decision-making—on all sorts of issues from water and waste management, transportation, and food production to upstream pollution seeping into downstream drinking water and urban populations moving into rural farming country. Isolationism and self-sufficiency at a local scale is simply impossible, like fingers trying to be independent of hand and body. Communication and information networks of all kinds would be—would need to be—maintained among the communities of a bioregion, and possibly some kind of political deliberative and decision-making body would eventually seem to be necessary.

The forms for such confederate bodies are myriad and their experiences rich and well-documented, so presumably working out the various systems would not be intractably difficult. We start, after all, with a clear identity of interest among these communities, a clear understanding of how they are interwoven into the bioregional tapestry, a clear historical record of their mutual needs and responsibilities and what happens when those are ignored. A confederation within bioregional limits has the logic, the force, of coherence and commonality; a confederation beyond those limits does not. Any larger political form is not only superfluous, it stands every chance of being downright dangerous, particularly in that it is no longer organically grounded in an ecological identity or limited by the constraints of homogeneous communities.

If, as the scholars suggest, the goal of government as we have now come to understand it in the 20th century is to provide liberty, equality, efficiency, welfare, and security in some reasonable balance, a strong argument can be made that it is the *areal* division of power, divided and subdivided again as in bioregional governance, that provides them best. It promotes *liberty* by diminishing the chances of arbitrary government action and providing more points of access for the citizens, more points of pressure for affected minorities. It enhances *equality* by assuring more participation by individuals and less concentration of power in a few remote and unresponsive bodies and offices. It increases *efficiency* by allowing government to be more sensitive and flexible, recognizing and adjusting to new conditions, new demands from the populace it serves. It advances *welfare* because at the smaller scales it is able to measure people's needs best and to provide for them more quickly, more cheaply, and more accurately.* And, because of all that, it actually improves *security* because, unlike the big and bumbling megastates vulnerable to instability and alienation, it fosters the sort of cohesiveness and allegiance that discourages crime and disruption within and discourages aggression and attack from without.

Even if we haven't modern experience to ratify it entirely, the logic certainly suggests that because bioregional governance stands in a direct and vital relation to the natural environment and its resources, and because it can deal with a population of cultural and ecological homogeneity, it can do more effectively for the populace those things that governments are supposed to do. But let us extend that logical process one more step.

· · ·

The ecological—and logical—corollary to the law of centrifugal force is the law of complementarity, or mutuality, under which the members of a single species within an econiche act

*Those who doubt that government is most effectively transmitted through smaller units might reflect on these figures: while there are 51 governments in the US ostensibly set up to solve the people's problems, the actual business of providing services in America (transportation, housing, fire protection, water power, etc.) is in the hands of more than 28,733 (in 1982) special-district governments at regional and local levels—*more than 500 times more small governments than large.* And even the national government, when it actually gets down to caring for its citizens' needs and desires, divides itself into some 1,460 general- and special-purpose organizations, and their number increases every year.

97

reciprocally and nonhierarchically to promote and defend their community. It is known among ecologists as "hetarchy," standing in conspicuous distinction to hierarchy, and signifies the idea of *distinction without rank*, an acknowledgment that blue is clearly different from yellow but not superior. Just as it makes no sense to think of the hierarchy of the parts of a tree—the bark better than the roots, say, and they higher in some way than the leaves—so it makes no sense to try to find rulers and ruled or lords and serfs within the animal subgroups—families, bands, hives, troops, flocks, or whatever. What we see, rather, are *complementary* roles, no one superior to any other, all necessary for the survival of the group. In the hive, for example, some are foragers, others fighters, some are egg-layers, others builders, and no sense of dominance or primacy among them exists. The queen bee, after all, is only a prodigious reproductive organ temporarily servicing the hive, and "queen" only because we designate her so, a title the drones and workers might have quite different ideas about. And so it is with the other labels from our political vocabulary used to describe certain animals—"dominant" males, "king of the hill," "ruling castes," "slaves," "workers," and the like—which really say more about Western culture than about animal behavior.

In fact, stratification and hierarchy within specific subgroups in the animal world is extremely rare, and almost all "evidence" of it is anthropomorphic carelessness. It is quite true that there are examples of aggressiveness and coercion in some mammalian groups—baboons, for example, wolves, mountain sheep—by certain males the ethologists call "alpha" males, and there may be conflict, particularly during mating periods, in which one individual wins sexual or territorial privileges over others. But even then there is no regular, organized, *institutionalized* system deserving of the word "hierarchy." These are, rather, individual acts of assertiveness by selected animals seeking the best for themselves in groups where space happenstantially opens up for them, where they perceive themselves as having the chance to make their lives easier or fuller. There is never such a thing as a troop "election" or ritualized behavior that would signify anything so formal as hierarchy or stratification, fixed orders and ranks and echelons. As Murray Bookchin puts it in his important philosophical study, *The Ecology of Freedom*, "The seemingly hierarchical traits of many animals are more like variations in the links of a chain than organized stratifications of the kind we find in human societies and institutions."*

And so it is also in the traditional societies, the preliterate cultures, as near as we can reconstruct them. There are seldom any of those "organized stratifications" we have become accustomed to in the industrialized world and almost never anything that even hints of dictatorship or monocracy. Like trees and beehives, such societies do not have structures of hierarchy and domination, and indeed create customs and taboos and rituals to *prevent* just such arrangements from disrupting the group. There are different roles, different specializations, sometimes varied by sex, sometimes by strength, sometimes by simple skill; but the roles complement each other, and although the individuals may gain status and admiration for particular successes, they do not occupy higher or lower po-

*It is worth noting, too, that the groups with alpha males are quite exceptional in nature. Though they are certainly found among baboons, in the more human-like great apes—gibbons, orangutans, chimpanzees, gorillas—they are extremely rare, and such behavior would be distinctly idiosyncratic. Gibbons, for example, almost always live in troops with the utmost egalitarianism, where sharing food among the entire aggregate is normal, and the roles of food-gatherer and baby-sitter are traded routinely between male and female.

sitions among their colleagues. The man adept at hunting seals, the woman favored as the singer of lullabies, the elder given the knowledge of magic, the grandmother wise in the healing power of herbs, the youth capable of leadership in battle—these are all important people and highly regarded, but they do not generally accumulate *power* to themselves as a result of their prowess, are not given positions on a ladder of command and dominance.

The story of Geronimo is wonderfully telling in this regard. He was a brave and able warrior, successful in several battles against the Mexicans and respected as a military leader; but he was not a "chief," for there was no such thing among the Apaches, and he never was accorded political stature or indeed any role of command off the battlefield. And when after one successful skirmish he tried to set himself up as a permanent tribal leader, he was promptly rejected and in fact cast out of the tribe, so he wandered the Arizona hills with a small band of brigands and raiders for most of the next twenty years. "He attempted to turn the tribe into the instrument of his desire," writes cultural anthropologist Pierre Clastres, who studied the Apaches, "whereas before, by virtue of his competence as a warrior, he was the tribe's instrument."

So why is he named in the history books as "a chief of the Apaches"? Because the white immigrants, in their cultural straitjackets, assumed that anyone who led a company of raiders against them must be a person of political power, the Indian equivalent of King Arthur or Richard I, and so applied to him their usual unthinking title for "savage" rulers: no more than that. The Apaches not only had no such position as chief, they had no form of governmental organization or even established political power. Clastres says of them, as of the numerous similar tribes he studied: "One is confronted, then, by a vast constellation of societies in which the holders of what elsewhere would be called power are actually without power; where the political is determined as a domain beyond coercion and violence, beyond hierarchical subordination; where, in a word, no relationship of command-obedience is in force."

. . .

The lessons of the law of complementarity from the animal world and traditional societies seem obvious enough as applied to a bioregional polity. Hierarchy and political domination would have no place; systems of ruler-and-ruled, even of elected-president-and-electing-people, are nonecological. So at the community level most decisions affecting people's daily lives would be both made and carried out by those with competence and experience in this task or that service, guided by the voice of the body as a whole and the principles of ecology. No leader, no ruling committee, no oligarchy, only citizens performing necessary roles: perhaps community officers for the accepted political functions—a magistrate, a treasurer, a sheriff, a facilitator, a clerk—and perhaps even a rotating series of coordinators, or archons, or managers. But these are people not with special *power*, only special *functions*, acting in complement and directed by the policies established by the community at large, routinely responsible to that community. Power, if it is to be found and named at all, rests only with the totality of the citizenry, not with any office.

Such a community of complementarity asks of its citizens a good deal of responsibility, of course, because where there is no one decision-maker, decision-making must be shared and assumed by everyone. It would be incumbent upon each individual to be willing to act as a public person, to be inquisitive and informed about public matters, to care and decide about public policies. This does not mean that every citizen has to be an expert on every subject or that there is no place in the polity for specialists. Indeed, in any complex community, we assume there would be some people who just know a lot more about cost accounting or waste management or soil restoration than others; that is precisely the undergirding assumption of complementarity in the first place. Shared responsibility means, rather, that the concerned citizen is involved enough and cares enough to decide which specialists to trust, with what, when, and how far.

Now I am under no illusions that such a condition is necessarily easy to establish, especially since it has been the fixed intention of the nation-state throughout its history to prevent the general exercise of that political responsibility. Even in those liberal countries such as the United States that pride themselves upon "democracy" and "universal suffrage," basic political responsibility has always been held in only a few hands. It was the precise intention of America's Founding Fathers, as of other aristocracies, not to let too many people of too many backgrounds mess around with the affairs of state, for these are best left to those who are competent to decide for others, to the educated and the expert, to the cool-headed and far-seeing. This intent, far from being washed away by the extension of the vote and other constitutional changes, has in fact been strengthened by the modern state, concerned with the theoretical efficiency of centralization and the theoretical strength of bureaucratic control. By now effective power has been almost totally drained from regions, states, cities, and towns, leaving them fewer and fewer decisions of meaning while more and more matters of substance (especially of taxation, finance, regulation, defense, and planning) are concentrated in the legislatures and bureaucracies of the capitals. A measure of the efficiency of this process is that even in such an open and free-wheeling nation as America, which makes a great deal of "citizenship" and "participation" and the like, the

very simplest expression of political responsibility—voting—
is undertaken by not much more than half the eligible voters,
and in the case of local elections, since the purpose seems to
them so trivial, by not much more than a fifth.

Thus to posit a bioregional politics that depends on the responsibility of true citizenship—that is, interested individuals regularly and willingly participating in all aspects of the
ongoing deliberations of the community—may seem to defy
history and even to run contrary to human experience. But
that is nonsense. Societies in all parts of the world in all periods of history have lived by the principles of political responsibility—that is in fact the way they survived. Their people *had* to concern themselves with the affairs of the polity,
with settling disputes between families, allocating the hind-
quarters of the mastodon, deciding when to plant the corn.
Citizenship was and had to be taken for granted, and communal decision-making was a necessity built into the life of
the community.

By the time of the Athenian Greeks it had even risen to the
state of an understood, an accepted, duty: *moira* meant the
inevitable, natural performance of duties to the polis in return
for all that the polis provided. *Duties*: this is not a question of
discretion or choice, an individual deciding whether or not to
vote; this is the customary, unquestioned, necessary way to
behave, and the Greek tragedies are mostly about what consequences attend those who shirk. As Pericles said of his fellow
Athenians: "We regard a man who takes no interest in public
affairs not as a harmless, but a *useless*, character." Participation was the citizen's obligation, and those who refused it had
no better status than aimless dogs pissing in the agora.

Where all individuals are citizens, involved in the *civitas*,
the true powers of complementarity are revealed. The strong
hues and delicate tints, the bold splashes and slender lines, the

full range of color and value, of shape and pattern, are evident in the canvas of a community's civic life, all parts contributing to the smoothness, the strength, even the magnificence of the whole. There is no meaning, no value, to hierarchy here; it would only be stifling and enervating, scorned as the impediment to community that it is.

· · ·

One last principle, simple and inevitable, must follow: the law of diversity. A healthy ecosystem usually tends toward diversity, and diversity usually means stability: a setback or calamity for one species in a fragile system of only ten is much more debilitating than in a system of several hundred—it could even lead to the system's overall collapse—which is why a temperate forest is likely to be more stable and recover from calamity more quickly than a subarctic tundra. In an ecosystem without centralization and hierarchy, where the natural tendencies to centrifugality and diffusion have full play, diversity and complexity of both animal and plant species are the inevitable consequences.

There's a nice story about the eminent British biologist J. B. S. Haldane that bears on this point. Once at a luncheon at an Oxford college he was asked, amid a group of distinguished theologians, what he thought was the principal characteristic of the Supreme Being of the universe, since after all he had spent a long lifetime examining the Almighty's manifestations on earth. The old man thought for a moment, bent forward and said: "An inordinate fondness for beetles."

The theologians were no doubt taken aback, but the answer, it turns out, is eminently reasonable; of the million or so animal species that have so far been identified, nearly half—some 400,000 of them—are beetles, far more than any other kind of animal. Such diversity in a single order is astonishing, almost unimaginable, and whether or not the Supreme Being can be said to have such a passion in fact, there is no doubt that the setting of the natural world obviously favors multiplicity and multiformity of that kind.

But beetles aside, the human animal in its own way is also a good example of the success of diversity. Neither so fertile as some species, so hardy or long-lived as others, it has survived these millions of years because it became adaptable. As a species we learned to climb trees *and* swim rivers, to run across prairies *and* swing on vines, to hunt and forage *and* to plant and nurture, to work alone like a hawk *and* in bands like wolves, to communicate intimately like honeybees *and* signal over great distances like porpoises, to know the world by smell *and* by three-dimensional sight, an acute sense of hearing, and a delicate sense of touch. Specialization works for the simplest species, microbes and bacteria, but it is this elaborate complexity, this variety of skills and roles, this unending polymorphism, that marks the human individual.

The same is true as well for the human *group*. From the start, the diverse and multi-skilled band was the more successful, and obviously the ones that learned fire-tending and tool-making and game-hunting and skin-wearing and food-storage were most adept at survival. And today, for the same reasons, the human organizations that perform best—businesses that survive longest, universities that prosper, cities that thrive decade after decade—are those that are differentiated and diversified, capable of adjusting to new circumstances and accomplishing many kinds of tasks. The ones that become unadaptable and rigid, overspecialized and uniform, are short-lived.

In this contemporary world, though the complexities of global societies sometimes seem dazzling, the unmistakable trend is toward uniformity and monolithicity in cultural as well as economic and political spheres. Trend is not destiny, as they say, but no one who has been to the Cairo Hilton or the airport at Kuala Lumpur, or who has had to deal with the bureaucrats in Nairobi or Bogota or Ottawa, or who has seen the jean-and-tee-clad youths of Warsaw or Ouagadougou or Waikiki, or who has eaten the food on an airline of any nation, can doubt the rapid and effective cocacolonization of much of the world in a mere quarter-century. Industrial culture, in the name of efficiency or modernity or economy, seeks uniformity, interchangeability, routinization, and conformity; it works toward one language, one currency, one bourse, one government, one measuring system, one kind of popular music, one style of medicine, one design of office block, one type of university. The tide seems well-nigh unstanchable and its signs are everywhere: whole nations given over to a single product, cities to a single industry, farms to a single crop, factories to a single article, people to a single job, jobs to a single motion.

That is the way not of stability but of precariousness, not of empowerment but of slavery, not of health but of sickness.

In a bioregional world, particularly one based on self-sufficiency and decentralization, the whole movement of the culture would naturally run in the opposite direction. Diversity would almost be a necessity for survival, within a community, within a city of communities, within a bioregion, within a continent, although clearly the types of diversity would need to change according to the scale. Different bioregions would inevitably move in different ways, develop different resources, find different forms of governance; and so, too, might different communities even within a bioregion, because they would have different settings, different connections to the land, different people upon it. The patchwork would be quite varied—

even, to an outsider, crazy—but the whole would add up to a
cozy and coherent quilt.

. . .

Diversity, let us pause briefly to reflect, though one of those
easy lip-service concepts, is a complex and possibly problem-
atic phenomenon in real life, and it leads to conclusions not
always welcomed by those who embrace its obvious virtues.

Let us take a bioregion, say a watershed. A certain homogeneity would exist there simply because the ways of making
a living, of building houses, of raising crops would be likely to
be similar; the people would be likely to have developed over
the years a particularized culture, a special way of talking, a
regional cuisine, an idiosyncratic sense of humor, a distinctive
style of art. Yet a certain divergence would be bound to exist
there also—differences between urban and rural, say, or hill
folk and valley folk, or ranchers and farmers, or those on the
upstream currents and those on the harbor tides. For the most
part the differences would probably be tolerable and slight,
even beneficial as they are in an ecosystem, but this is the
point: even when those differences rub raw and real animos-
ities emerge, the diversity giving rise to them must be treasured and preserved. It would be the purpose of a bioregional
polity in its various forms to find agreement between quar-
relsome communities, of course, but agreement at the cost of
squelching variety or imposing uniformity comes at too high
a price: a certain tolerance is the inevitable concomitant of
diversity. As the stable econiche permits—even, in a sense,
encourages—a certain amount of disharmony and conflict,
appreciating that the interests of all species cannot be in agreement at all times, that disputes over territory or scavenging

rights or access to sunlight can exist, so the stable bioregion must do likewise.

Bioregional diversity, it must be understood, means exactly that. It does not mean that every community in a bioregion, every subregion within an ecoregion, every ecoregion on a continent, would construct itself along the same lines, evolve the same political forms. Most particularly it does not mean that every bioregion would be likely to heed the values of democracy, equality, liberty, freedom, justice, and the like, the sort that the liberal American tradition proclaims. Truly autonomous bioregions would inevitably go in separate and not necessarily complementary ways, creating their own political systems according to their own environmental settings and their own ecological needs.

Now any region true to bioregional principles would necessarily respect the limitations of scale, the virtues of conservation and stability, the importance of self-sufficiency and cooperation, and the desirability of decentralization and diversity—and one can only imagine that these principles would impel its polity in the direction of libertarian, noncoercive, open, and more-or-less democratic governance. But of course they *need* not. Different cultures could be expected to have quite different views about what political forms could best accomplish their bioregional goals, and (especially as we imagine this system on a global scale) those forms could be at quite some variance from the Western Enlightenment–inspired ideal. And however much one might find the thought unpleasant, that divergence must be expected and—if diversity is desirable—respected. It is quite possible that an extraordinary variety of political systems would evolve within the bioregional constraints, and there is no reason to think that they would necessarily be compatible—or even, from someone else's point of view, *good*.

Gandhi remarks somewhere that it is worthless to go on "dreaming of systems so perfect that no one will need to be good." But that is exactly what I think *is* necessary: to imagine systems that will work even if the people in them are *not* good. There's not much point, it seems to me, in dreaming of systems where we expect everyone *will* be good. Not only would that be likely to produce a fairly vapid society, but the long history of human behavior suggests that such a system would not evolve on this planet no matter how long we have a go at it. What we must do is dream of systems that allow people to be *people*, in all their variousness—and that includes being wrong on occasion, and errant and even evil, to commit the crimes that as near as we know have always been committed— and *still* permit their communities, their societies to survive and prosper as close to climax stability as possible.

That means, first of all, systems where all civil and social structures work to minimize errant behavior—where, for example, an individual normally feels part of the web of nature and is accorded a particular role and value within it; where bonds of community are strong and social forms supportive and nurturing; where material needs and desires are for the most part fulfilled; where individual or even community actions transgressing bioregional standards are known to everyone and their unfortunate consequences visible to all; and where individual acts of violence or disharmony are perceived as contrary to both communal and ecological principles. That means, secondly, systems where such errant behavior can be channeled and compartmentalized, constricted by scale, so it cannot do irreparable damage beyond narrow physical limits; the evil-doer, whether an individual or a whole community, is thus held in check by the limits of bioregional decentralism and cannot send poisons coursing through the veins of entire continents and the world itself, as can happen in a global monoculture. Bioregionalism, properly conceived, provides just such systems.

Bioregionalism, then, not merely tolerates but thrives on the diversity of human behavior, and the varieties of political and social arrangements they give rise to, the way a laboratory thrives on multiple experiments or a scholarly institute on multiple disciplines. This diversity is the way to foster creativity and innovation, the dynamics of synergy, out of which eventually come the enhancements and advancements of life. It is the way to guard against the disasters that monocultures are open to, as when an entire citrus-planted valley falls prey to the Mediterranean fruit fly or an entire country succumbs to the potato blight. Diversity has its own special values, its own nurturant complexities, and it is to be welcomed even though at times it may give rise to the unwanted novelty, the unpleasant mutant, and even though in human systems it may allow those practices that stem from the baser rather than the nobler motives.

In any case, in the real world, there is no other way to have it.

EIGHT

Society

A FEW YEARS AGO when asked by *The New York Times* to name his choices for the seven wonders of the natural world, biologist Lewis Thomas led off with what he called the "extraordinary phenomenon" of the oncideres beetle and the mimosa tree.

It seems that when she wishes to lay her eggs the female oncideres beetle unfailingly picks out the mimosa tree from all others in the forest, crawls out on one of its limbs, and cuts a long lengthwise slit, into which she drops her egg sacs. Then, because in the larval stage the offspring cannot survive in live wood, she backs down the branch a foot or so and cuts a neat circular slit through the bark all around the limb. This has the effect of killing the branch within a very short time and eventually the dead wood succumbs to some strong wind and falls to the ground, where it remains as the home for the next generation of oncideres beetles as they hatch. But, interestingly, removing the limb also has the effect of pruning the mimosa tree, a rather valuable ancillary result because, left alone, a mimosa has a lifespan of just twenty-five to thirty years, but pruned in this simple way, it can flourish for a century or more.

Dr. Thomas seems to consider this relationship sufficiently unusual to be regarded as a wonder of the world, particularly worthy, he writes, because such things "keep reminding us of how little we know about nature." Well, of course confession on the side of ignorance is wise for humans in Gaean matters, I agree, and yet I think it is permissible to point out that, far from being unusual, this sort of biological interaction is in fact commonplace throughout nature.

The relationship is called *symbiosis*, and its persistence and pervasiveness in the natural world should suggest to us another fundamental law: on its most intimate scale nature favors symbiosis, interaction, mutual dependence as the means of survival. We see it at the microscopic level of the mitochondria that float about in our very cells, infinitesimal creatures with their own DNA and RNA which maintain and replicate themselves for as long as we are alive and without which we could not move or breathe. We see it at the level of the giant clam, that strange creature of the major oceans that becomes in a sense both animal *and* plant; it survives entirely through the photosynthetic action of the plant cells that it engulfs and actually incorporates into its body, and the plant cells survive because they are protected and nurtured by the clam—and have even induced it over time to evolve small lens-like tissues that focus sunlight like a magnifying glass and help enhance their photosynthesis.

And we see such symbiosis also in the usual human family, one of the most complex associations known in the animal world, in which the senior female often gives herself over for many years to birthing and a long period of suckling and tending, during which the senior male must act as the special provider and protector—all to nurture offspring who take more than a decade to mature and who are expected to return the favor of such tedious upbringing with support and provisioning in their parents' later years, and with a mysterious component that, if given, they may return, called love.

Dr. Thomas's astonishment to the contrary, then, symbiosis is essentially the way that nature has normally seen fit to work. Not all its forms are necessarily perceived as equitable by the participants, as we have seen with predation, but some mutuality is always there, a mutuality that has evolved over eons so that the species may survive. Indeed, if our contemporary understanding teaches anything at all, it is that species survive not because of any particular attribute of one of its "fittest" individuals, but because the population *as a whole* has evolved a mutual relationship with another species. In his speculative but shrewd little book, *Symbiosis*, biologist William Trager maintains that it is not necessarily any kind of *conflict* in nature that accounts for a species' success: "Few people realize that mutual cooperation between different kinds of organisms—symbiosis—is just as important, and that the 'fittest' may be the one that most helps another to survive."

So symbiosis is as apt a model as any for a successful human society, which we may envision as a place where families operate within neighborhoods, neighborhoods within communities, communities within cities, cities within regions, all on the basis of collaboration and exchange, cooperation and mutual benefit, and where the fittest is the one that helps the most—and of course is thereby the most helped.

. . .

The most important instance of such an interaction on a bioregional scale would be the social symbiosis between the city and the country, between the urban machine and the rural inflorescence, a correlation that has been celebrated by philosophers from Aristotle on. Fritz Schumacher, that wise and human economist, has said it as well as any of them:

> Human life, to be fully human, needs the city; but it also needs food and other raw materials gained from the country. Everybody needs ready access to both countryside and city. It follows that the aim must be a *pattern* of urbanization so that every rural area has a nearby city, near enough so that people can visit it and be back the same day. No other pattern makes human sense.
>
> Actual developments during the last hundred years or so, however, have been in the exactly opposite direction: the rural areas have been increasingly deprived of access to worthwhile cities. There has been a monstrous and highly pathological polarization of the pattern of settlements.

That polarization, producing a gulf between industrial and agricultural, sophisticated culture and native, users of resources and producers, the world of nature and the world of society, is exactly what a bioregional world would be organically designed to prevent. Following a symbiotic model, the goals would instead be to establish parity in the relationships between a city and its hinterlands, a mutual flow that recognizes the dependence—a needful, mutually understood dependence—of one upon the other.

On the one hand, the city would be necessary as the producer of certain kinds of goods, and Jane Jacobs has made it clear how the compact and interactive city can be particularly good as a *regional* engine, a heart, a fountain. It could be the efficient magnet for trade, providing the necessary marketplace not only for its own goods but for those produced in the surrounding countryside as well. It could with sufficient population sustain the specialized services, both public and private, that urban centers have traditionally provided: hospitals and libraries and symphonies, where those are thought to be desirable, and art restoration and sexual company and musical shows, where those are. It could be the center of "high" culture, at least of the familiar kind, providing the congress among artists and converse among poets that so often makes the enriched soil creativity demands. And it could provide, as did fit and textured cities of the past, an amalgam of those theoretical urban virtues—anonymity, complexity, tolerance, self-expression, stimulation—that are deficient or nonexistent in many rural and small-town settings.

On the other hand, the countryside, farm and nonfarm, would of course be necessary as the primary source of food and water and all the basic raw materials of shelter, clothing, manufacture, and artisanship upon which the city depends. It could be the place of memory, where those closest to the land remember the ways and carry on the traditions of the bioregion, so that the Gaean values are never lost and the urbanites may ever be reminded of ecological reality. It could be a source of its own kinds of creativity and innovation, its own crafts and artforms, its own styles of deliberation and intercourse, a different and earthier voice. And it could be the place of residence for the majority of the population, since the proportion deliberately favoring city life (as against those forced to it without choice) is likely to be as small in the future as opinion polls in the US have shown it to be in the past—roughly a quarter*—and a healthy ecosystem cannot in any case support very many cities.

Which brings us directly to the problem of population distribution, a social necessity if any sort of sound bioregional world is to come about. Giant cities, as we have seen, are eco-

*In general public opinion surveys indicate that only 10 percent of Americans prefer big cities, 10–15 percent prefer medium-sized cities, 30–40 percent prefer small towns within the orbit of a city, and 30–35 percent prefer small cities, small towns, and rural areas.

logically untenable because they must draw down resources beyond the carrying capacity of the land on which they rest. I've seen various population estimates, ranging from 25,000 to 250,000, as the maximum number for an ecological city— the variation of course depending on how much of its immediate arable land the city uses for food and biomass and how much it depends on the countryside—but informed opinion seems to agree that it is not possible to go much beyond that upper limit. That being the case, there seems to be no sensible choice but to break down the current multimillion-people cities both by dividing them into smaller cities, each with a surrounding greenbelt, and by resettling them into different-sized communities in the surrounding region.

Actually, contrary to common supposition, there are only 48 cities over 250,000 in the US, and they hold no more than a fifth of the total population. That number could be distributed in as many as 150 new cities with as much as 100 square miles for each—twice the current national average—and the amount of new space required would still be only a twelfth the size of Montana. Population relocation of this sort need not be all that difficult or disruptive, stretched over several decades and done with due regard for natural systems; as James L. Sundquist, author of the authoritative *Dispersing Population*, puts it: "A population dispersal policy and the programs to execute it can be conceived simply enough. They are likely to be popular. They are not unduly costly. And they work." Moreover, there is plenty of land for such dispersal in any bioregion in North America (certain European countries would have more difficulty, but their problems are by no means intractable). Even the surplus 5 million or so from New York City could be efficiently redistributed through the Hudson River georegion without any environmental impact beyond the range of recovery.

One further word about the symbiosis between city and country. As the giant clam takes on features of the plant cells it ingests, and as those cells become in some ways animal-like, so an effective relationship between urban and rural leads to a certain kind of social mix-and-match. The receptive hinterland might take on some of the compatible practices of the city: small towns, for example, could learn the virtues of density rather than sprawl in designing new buildings, especially for the elderly; a small city might appreciate the wisdom of setting aside a block or so of clubs and pubs for its young people as a place for necessary misbehavior; new towns created in the countryside could follow the example of urban clustering and become cohesive villages instead of imitating those towns with isolated farmhouses strung out for miles along a stretch of highway; and rural areas wanting to simulate the city's culture could establish networks of musicians for a symphony orchestra or networks of libraries (town and personal) for an extended and enriched book service. And so on and on, the ways of imitation being as infinite as those of urban life itself, the models being always there for the attentive village and town to learn from and borrow.

Similarly, for the attentive bioregional city, living on and with the earth would be a necessitarian matter of course, and the spirit of the countryside would need to become absorbed into the veins of the city. Not merely in the sense of parks and woodlands and greenswards and canals and waterways, as fundamental as they would be for any city to establish; not merely vest-pocket gardens and window boxes and treelined streets and fountained plazas, as desirable as they would be. But more: the city would have to be as rooted in the earth, as close to the natural processes, as the farm and the village. That would require growing much of its own food in backyard, rooftop, and community gardens or in a surrounding farm-belt; generating most of its own energy with wind machines and solar collectors; recycling its wastes, both organic and solid; making maximum use of trees and shrubs to absorb dirt, heat, and noise; designing transportation primarily for cyclists and pedestrians; constructing buildings of local materials, with energy efficiency, durability, and human use uppermost—in short, integrating into every urban process a total understanding of ecological principles that is at present so astonishingly lacking. By being continually in touch with the natural world, every citizen, even the tiniest child, would realize that water does not come from a pipe in the basement, and tomatoes do not grow on supermarket shelves, and you can't throw anything away because there is no "away."

. . .

The long, slow process by which symbiosis comes about and is maintained in the biotic world suggests another principle of importance for human social arrangements: the law of *homeorrhesis*, or stabilized flow, measured change, evolutionary adjustment.

Now nature of course is not pacific and it is not without cataclysms of considerable violence: those who have seen Mount St. Helens in its dramatic eruptions or an October tropical hurricane sweep across the Florida Keys know the huge and unpredictable power of the living earth. But in most ecosystems its usual mien, its general day-to-day style, is one of gradualness and regularity, slowness and steadiness, as careful and as measured as the progress of tectonic plates or the movements of a turtle; and its long-term tempos are elegantly deliberate, measured by eons, with a careful, unhastened kind of evolution that takes a million years to fashion an enlarged brain and a thousand years to define a river's granite-bounded course.

It is not change, then, and it is not novelty or rapidity that the bioregional society works toward but rather stability and adjustment; not revolution but evolution; not cataclysm but gradualism. The new is to be treated more with suspicion than, as in our time, instant acclaim and approbation—the mutant being always more likely to cause problems than solve them—and no particular virtue would adhere to originality or "modernity," as it does in a society with no fixed and accepted standards, no repository of values from the past, to measure by. Adopting change for change's sake—or for variety's or amusement's or greed's—is simply anti-ecological, antithetical to the functional processes of nature. The rapid introduction of new styles and "fashions" in consumer goods of all kinds, of new movies and programs and "personalities," of new works of art and culture with every season and every star, may suit a society where some 13,000 new products are thrust on supermarket and drugstore shelves every single year, but it is obviously bewildering, unstabilizing, and undesirable in a settled system where forms of social intercourse, culture, and taste have been worked out slowly over the years. Innovation and a sort of fine-tuning can have their place, but as a response to necessity rather than as whim or novelty.

The overall character of a bioregional society, therefore, is directed by images of sustenance and maintenance, the slow healing and mending behavior of all living things, rather than those of alteration and inconstancy, which are usually the signs of damage and disease.

In this light it is also possible to look at crime and violence in an ecological way, as symptoms of excessively rapid change or social instability, for they are most prevalent in societies characterized by rampant growth and turbulence, such as ours. In an ecological society crime, as either an individual act or a social trend, is that which transgresses the law of homeorrhesis. Greatest opprobrium, and presumably punishment, would attend those acts that are most violent and disruptive, that cause severe or permanent damage to the ecosystem, no matter what supposed economic or material benefits they may offer—such as murder or clearcutting or species extinction or the introduction of the gypsy moth.* Least disfavor would fall upon the least disruptive acts and those that do not violate fundamental ecological principles—such as burglary or vagrancy or drunkenness.

Of course the entire moral structure of an ecologically conscious society would rest on Gaean principles. Oughts and Shoulds would not be based primarily on protecting private property or personal wealth or individual achievement, as in Western morality, but on securing bioregional stasis and environmental equilibrium. It would be "wrong" in such a society to urinate in five gallons of water and flush it into a river, to use chemical fertilizers, to build a skyscraper or a mall or any energy-wasteful building, to eat high on the food chain day after day, to devote a farm to a single crop, to burn or discard organic garbage, to be ignorant of the phrases "carrying capacity" and "biotic community." Something of the same moral weight would attach to more conventional

---

*The gypsy moth was introduced into the United States from Europe in the 1860s by a New England entrepreneur who hoped to cross this fast-breeding species with the silk moth to produce an abundant crop of silkworms to make him rich. Not only did the new species not successfully take to the crossbreeding, it went and escaped from the laboratory—and then, since it is both highly prolific and highly undiscriminating, willing to feed on more than 500 species of trees and shrubs, it began to devastate the countryside. Because there were no existing predators on this continent to control the moths and few species willing to take on the job, the devastation has remained unchecked to this date, amounting to more than 2 million acres a year and now extending from Maine to Virginia and west to Wisconsin.

crimes—killing, mugging, rustling, rioting, and the like—
that would bring disfavor not because there are statutes and
codes against them but because they are seen and felt to be
disruptive of the normal social flow of the community, threatening its success and even survival as a self-reliant unit.

. . .

The ultimate form of disruption in any society, the ultimate
transgression of homeorrhesis, is of course warfare. As a fact
of life—perhaps even bioregional life—we must look at it
squarely.

Despite all I have indicated previously about the essentially
quiet and benign pattern of the ecosystem in its mature, climax state, it is also true that aggression and occasionally what
looks very much like war within a species do exist in the animal realm, particularly in the vertebrate subphylum, and they
exist as well among a great many tribal societies. Aggression
appears to be an ecological instinct in some sense, since it performs certain clear functions in animal communities: it serves
to distance certain communities in an ecorealm from each
other, for example, thus helping match the population to the
carrying capacity of the territory; and war itself serves to limit
populations absolutely. Therefore what we generally see in
the natural world is not an attempt to *eliminate* aggression and
battle—that is a misguided dream of pacifists—but to *minimize* it, to limit it, to ritualize it, to channel it, so that it does
not cause fundamental disruption. For the bioregional society
the homeorrhetic goal would be not so much to do away with
every form of aggression as to make it predictable and routine,
to control it so that its damaging effects are reduced.

The ways that might be available to a stable bioregion to
provide harmony within and protection from without would
be varied indeed, and it is probably impossible to try to imag-

ine them all. But we can get some idea of their range and compass by reflecting on what have historically been the kinds of reasons for human aggression and finding ways a bioregional society might accommodate or minimize or even eradicate them.

One must perforce start with the relationship of a society to its environment. I believe the work of Karl Wittvogel and Lewis Mumford, supplemented by the explorations of the Frankfurt School and, especially, Murray Bookchin, give ample evidence that, in brief, societies that dominate nature also dominate people. Where there is the idea that a massive dam should be built to control a river's flow, there is the idea that people should be enslaved to build it; where there is the belief that a giant metropole may serve itself by despoiling the surrounding countryside and devouring its raw materials, there are castes and hierarchies to ensure that this is accomplished; and where there is the philosophy that a society has the right to exert its control over the plants and animals around it, using them as it can to its own maximal benefit, there is the philosophy of warfare which merely extends to other humans the privileges accorded the rest of the biota.

The bioregional society, as we have sketched it thus far, would be patently quite different from any of this. As it understands itself to dwell in the land, to be a part of the Gaean web of life and form, it would be guided by a spirit not of dominance but humility, not of control-over but harmony-within, not of being empowered but being privileged. And to that extent, its interest in and capacity for warfare would be slim indeed.

But as we know, even certain human groups with perspectives as near to Gaean as we can imagine have succumbed to war. Not to oversimplify, but the ample record does suggest, for tribal societies anyway, that this tends to happen for two reasons: when a population grows beyond its stable limits and wants new land occupied by others, or when there is a competition for scarce resources or sudden deprivation of an outside resource on which it depended. Happily, neither condition need obtain in a bioregional society as carefully attuned to its environment as contemporary skills and knowledge permit. If it knew anything, a bioregion would know its carrying capacity and the limit of the population it could sustain, and all social strictures would be bent to assure that the folly of overshoot was avoided; and, if it were essentially self-sufficient, it would know through sheer daily existence how to survive on its own resources and avoid dependence on or competition for outside supplies of any kind. Above all, one would suppose, a steady-state bioregion, no matter how amply endowed, simply would not under normal conditions find it *economical* to divert its time and materiel from daily sustenance into preparing and waging war, or divert its much-needed human labor from farms and shops into barracks and trenches.

To be sure, there are other causes of war than the need for space or plunder, but they tend to be reflections of an aberrant or exceedingly unsettled society. For example, the whims of an idle dictator or warrior caste, or their need to occupy the subject hordes with something other than plans for rebellion; or, in a more modern vein, the desire of the nation-state to strengthen itself by creating a jingo-patriotism among its populace and enlarging its powers of force and control as it can do in wartime—war being, in Randolph Bourne's famous phrase, "the health of the state." Or, similarly, the need of a tribe or nation that is socially awry and contentious within itself, without outlets for aggression through the games and rituals of its daily life, to force its malignancies outward and, by warfare, transpose its inner violence onto its neighbors.

Whatever variation there may be among them, bioregional

societies with any degree at all of ecoconsciousness would be unlikely to exhibit this sort of behavior. If they paid any attention at all to ecological laws, their entire social purpose would be stability and harmony, developing the means by which their members would be, in contemporary terms, "effectively socialized," without any particular need for violence and disruption and with supportive communal ties that mitigate individual aberrance. And if that were not sufficient to contain the aggressive instinct, they would be led to develop ways to canalize and deflect and control it: sport, for example, is a classic means, as with lacrosse among the Creek Indian tribes or soccer among Italian cities, and so is ritual combat, as in the knightly lists.

But then, even assuming the majority of bioregional societies were essentially peaceful, with no more interest in conquest and war than the hickory or the hedgehog, suppose there was just one wrong-headed society, just one bioregion that for some reason became an aggressive anomaly—what then? As Andrew Smookler puts it in his pessimistic "parable of the tribes": "What if all but one choose peace, and that one is ambitious for expansion and conquest? What can happen to the others when confronted by an ambitious and potent neighbor?" In Smookler's view they can submit or fight or run away or, most likely, imitate the aggressor; there are no other choices. The end result must be a most unecological disruption of homeorrhesis, indeed what seems to be a nearly permanent state of contestation and warfare, every tribe at each other's throat or planning to be and all given over to hatred and suspicion and disputation.

That may be, we moderns are tempted to think, the true condition of humankind, and it certainly resembles the ghastly Armageddon-in-being the 20th century has so far managed to accustom us to. But it is, to begin with, a profound misreading of the archeological and anthropological record. In fact, warfare among hunter-gatherer and nomadic tribes seems to have been extremely rare and the prospect of it to have led to innumerable institutions and customs designed either to prevent its outbreak or, once begun, to minimize its effect—through strong taboos against general slaughter (as, for example, among the Plains Indians) or through ritualized opportunities for one-on-one combat among leaders (as, for example, David and Goliath). Moreover, even in historical times the unmistakable pattern of settled societies has generally been one of tolerance rather than hostility, trade rather than plunder, isolation rather than conquest—and if it is Genghis Khan and Chaka Zulu and Julius Caesar that we choose to remember and, with a certain tremble, glorify, that describes our militaristic mentalities far more than the historical reality. And, with several notable exceptions when all social norms broke down, the rules and proscriptions of war in most of these societies were normally so elaborate as to diminish its costs and casualties, at least until the 19th century, to something rather less than an average week in the streets and bars of Manhattan.

Beyond that, it is important to see the ways in which a bioregional society might operate to frustrate the "inevitable" conflicts suggested by the "parable of the tribes." Being relatively small, bioregions would in general be insufficiently powerful to launch and sustain serious warfare, which is after all the stuff of empires and nation-states (and the larger the state, the greater the casualties of war, as I have elsewhere proved), not of territories composed of self-regarding communities. Being small, they would similarly offer little in the way of reward for the outside invader, and such riches as they might have could be obtained by barter or agreement far more easily and economically than by war.

And, being healthy, independent, self-reliant entities, the bioregions would offer much in the way of resistance. This means, of course, an active concept of defense—with citizens armed and trained to serve in community militias (all ages, both sexes) and educated in sophisticated forms of civilian resistance (both passive and active) in the case of attack—making any bioregion an extremely unpleasant nettle, an unwelcome scorpion, for any prospective invader, very much in the way that Switzerland has proved to be during the last 500 years. Indeed no deterrent, no defense, can compare with the union of proud and motivated citizens standing shoulder to shoulder in defense of the territory they know and love, that they have become true dwellers in, fiercely joined in all those attributes of a bioregional society the Pentagon's computers can never reckon: cooperation, self-sacrifice, community morale, patriotism, neighborliness. "There is no barrier," Gladstone once said, "like the breast of free men"—and, in the bioregional militia, women—and any hostile force, no matter how powerful, would learn that quickly.*

The means for war between bioregions, therefore, would be limited, the rewards more limited still, the necessity quite nonexistent. In such conditions it is not woolly-headed to

---

*Similarly, in the instance that always seems to crop up, of the Russians deciding to invade a bioregional North America (assuming they were not similarly bioregional and for some reason wanted to bother). One can imagine a hostile Russia waging war against a unified and centralized United States, hoping to defeat the official army, occupy the official capital, replace the official administration with its own. It is much harder to imagine Russia wanting to send its forces valley by valley, hill by hill, across a continent of autonomous bioregions, each with armed and motivated militias, none with a centralized apparatus to conquer and control (nor is there a continental one), all of them determined to defend the econiches they have learned and loved.

imagine a general state of undisrupted homeorrhesis—or, as we might make so bold to call it, peace.

And if the clash should come, if for some reason bioregion were set against bioregion, the model of most animal aggression suggests the ways to limit its human and environmental effects. Two rattlesnakes in battle, though the bite of either is quite deadly, do not bite; they tangle and twine and wrestle— it actually looks something like thumb-wrestling—one trying to lay its upper body across the other's neck; and when one holds the other submissive for a moment the battle is over, the loser slinks away, and conquest is achieved without cost. Two oryx antelopes in battle, each equipped with long pointed horns capable of ripping a lion's belly, may butt and push and kick and knock antlers in ritualistic enmity, but never do they use their horns to spear and gouge each other, not even when the one exhausted first succumbs and falls, acknowledging loss. Thus two bioregions in battle, knowing as they do the ways of nature around them, could contrive to make their warfare serious and meaningful without making it necessarily deadly, rapacious, or permanently disruptive—a means of making even warfare, if we can imagine this, more like adjustment than convulsion.

· · ·

There is one last principle that also bears on the stability and harmony of a bioregional society, derived both from the biological world, where it is a means of assuring health, and the human experience, where it has been a means of preventing war: division.

When seeking salubrity and balance, it is nature's way to divide rather than to unite, to move toward smaller units rather than larger. As economist Leopold Kohr has written in his careful discussion of this phenomenon:

> If smallness represents nature's mysterious principle of health, and bigness its principle of disease, *division* . . . must of necessity represent its principle of cure. . . . Division (or multiplication, which exerts a similar reducing effect on the size of things) represents not only the principle of cure but of progress. . . . The only way of restoring a healthy balance to the world's diseased conditions seems thus . . . through the division of those social units which have outgrown manageable proportions.

Division is the underlying principle of all animal cells, the principle of growth. The power of the human brain comes from its multiple million-cell divisions; the power of the human species from its multiple and varied cultures and languages that divided off from a common stock millions of years ago, a diversity found in no other mammal. As books are improved by division into chapters, houses into rooms, and ships into compartments, so human societies are improved by division into regions—a natural phenomenon found in all cultures—and regions into areas and cities into communities.

The principle is especially important applied to human affairs because, whatever contemporary wheelers and dealers may think, the capacity of the human brain is limited and the ability of human ingenuity in self-governance is limited. Just as everything in nature grows but then at its fit and determined size *stops* growing, so human societies have a fit and determined size at which human faculties can cope best, and beyond which they should reasonably stop growing. The size may vary somewhat according to the conditions of the environment (a temperate forest is more hospitable than a desert) or the particular abilities of that set of individuals, but after some optimum limit the societies will get caught in an inevitable bind. As anthropologist William Rathje has formulated it, as the size of a population doubles, its state of complexity—the information exchanged, the decisions required, the controls necessary, the readjustments needed—*quadruples*, and the problems of stability and harmony thus grow far faster than the capacities of human talents to solve them. Where the growth curves cross, some sort of division—separation, segmentation, fission, resettlement, partition—is obviously desirable.

This is of course the principle by which many societies have maintained peace and harmony through history. Early tribal societies worked always within understood limits—often around 500 people or so, that basic *village* size I suggested earlier—and, when they exceeded those bounds, would encourage a small band or family to go off and find its own watering hole and establish its own village. Greek city-states maintained their limited scope—generally no more than 8,000 to 10,000 people or so, the *tribal* size suggested earlier—by segmentation and often by establishing new colonies on suitable islands or upland valleys. New England towns of the 18th century continually split and resettled, either within the boundaries of the township itself (one reason, for example, for the presence of three or four Congregational churches in a single Massachusetts village) or farther up the mountain or down the river (one reason for such a characteristic settlement pattern of small towns and cities in the region). And Switzerland has maintained its extraordinary long record of peace and harmony by clinging firmly to the idea of cantonal divisions—separations which, like everything else there, are taken seriously—and even to the practice of subdividing one contentious canton into two separate units when necessary.

The obviousness of the idea of division as a social solvent is of course obscured by the power of nation-states to propound national unity and patriotic togetherness, but it has been convincingly put forward by any number of recent writers, most notably among them Lewis Mumford, E. F. Schumacher, and Leopold Kohr. Jane Jacobs, that astute philosopher of cities, recently put the case in her *Cities and the Wealth of Nations*, arguing the need for some sort of "radical discontinuity" for nations caught in an unhalting economic decline:

> The radical discontinuity would thus be the division of the single sovereignty into a family of smaller sovereignties, not after things had reached a stage of disintegration but long before, while things were still going reasonably well. In a society behaving like this, multiplication of sovereignties by division would be a normal, untraumatic accompaniment to economic development, and to the increasing complexity of economic and social life. Some of the sovereignties in the family would in their turn divide, as evidence of the need to do so appeared. A nation behaving like this would substitute for one great life force, sheer survival, that other great life force, reproduction.

Jacobs calls all this "theoretical" and doesn't seem to think it has much of a chance to be enacted in the present world, but she does cite the examples of Norway's division from Sweden and Singapore's from Malaysia; to which we might add the separation of Belgium from France, Bangladesh from Pakistan, Albania from Turkey, Austria from Hungary, and, in slightly different circumstances, North Korea from South, and West Germany from East. Whatever the vast differences among them, the one obvious truth is that division at this level at least does *not* lead to collapse and stagnation for the separated states. On the contrary, it seems to allow room for new energies and abilities to develop and thrive.

For a bioregion, the principle of division might reasonably apply at two different levels.

First, for bioregional cities conscious of carrying capacities, division would be the obvious way to regulate population, either by physically dividing up the city into two or more sub-cities or by inducing some segments of the population to move to new areas. Voluntary resettlement, as the experience in several European countries has shown, is not a difficult social policy to carry out, particularly since a great many people prefer to live outside large cities and welcome a chance at having new jobs and new homes. In a bioregional setting, where developing rural areas for farms and small towns would be a top priority, and where living close to the earth would presumably be a Gaean preference, it should be extremely easy and natural.

Second, for a large bioregion encountering increasingly intractable problems as the population expands or cultures grow apart, dividing into smaller bioregions would be a natural way to rechannel and refocus energies and see to the revivification of neglected areas. An ecoregion might very easily divide into several morphoregions over time, especially where the character of the environment generates different kinds of human economies and cultures that someday might feel the need to declare their own distinctiveness. I could imagine, for example, that the physical features of the estuary of the Hudson River—not to mention the special nature of a rather large city at its mouth—would eventually lead it to develop a bioregional society somewhat different from that of the upper Hudson Valley, and that the single georegion could be divided into two perfectly compatible but separate—and stronger—ones. The process is perfectly organic and thoroughly ecological.

I remember once, discussing the question of areal division with Leopold Kohr, I kept probing him, challenging him with this hypothesis and that. Finally he leaned to me and said, "I've been trying to find an image that will make it clear to you. I see it now. Think of trying to carry water across a room in a long shallow dish whose sides are no bigger than an inch tall. What would happen? You would spill most of it before you got halfway across. And that," he ended with a triumphant twinkle, "is why they invented *ice trays*, whose very success is based on the idea that by dividing things you make them manageable."

. . .

I am tempted to go on discussing the bioregional paradigm forever, to explore what agriculture would look like in a bioregional world, for example, to examine in detail the construction of commodious cities, to outline the ways of bioregional health, and education, and transportation, and energy, and courtship, and much else besides. But that of course is beyond my scope, probably beyond my competence, and best left in the hands of the bioregional citizenry, when it evolves, to undertake for itself, with study, in depth, over time. I trust that in delving into just these four broad areas—scale, economy, polity, and society—I have suggested the basics of that bioregional paradigm, some of the bones, a little of the meat, so that we may be able to give some life to the bioregional vision.

III

The Bioregional Project

At bottom, the problems of American regionalism are the problems of American civilization: the continuous process of bringing to fruition the best of which American men and women are capable.

Felix Frankfurter, *Regionalism in America*

Only if we know *that we have actually descended into* infernal regions *where nothing awaits us but "the cold death of society and the extinguishing of all civilised relations," can we summon the courage and imagination needed for a "turning around," a* metanoia. *This then leads to seeing the world in a new light, namely, as a place where the things modern man continuously talks about and always fails to accomplish* can actually be done.

E. F. Schumacher, *A Guide for the Perplexed*

· NINE ·

Past Realities

OVER THE YEARS I have been assembling a file, quite sizable now, that for want of a better description I have called "How to Get." It is the file into which I put all the various strategies I come across for ways to change the world, petty and grandiose, feasible and foolish, successful and hopeless, and its label is a shorthand for the question I am often asked at public lectures: "Your vision seems plausible enough, and your world sounds as if it might possibly be a better one and probably what we need to save us all—but *how do we get from this world to that?*"

It is a question that has no exact answer, of course, because no one knows or ever could know, and the conditions that give rise to sweeping social change differ not just from century to century and place to place but virtually from moment to moment, a swirl of possibilities as unpredictable as the winds. Moreover, it contains a profound paradox, for the question is precisely a product of a scientistic world—*this* world—that likes its programs set and routes given and answers supplied. Anyone who asks it has not yet come to understand that there is no one solution, no single path to a bioregional world—*that* world—and the process of getting there is not one of linear neatness, as in computers, but of organic diversity, as in life.

But there is pertinence to that question, nonetheless. It speaks to that acute and decided need in the contemporary world for a political project of worth and meaning, some serious way not merely to think of but to *achieve* alternatives. As such, it deserves to be addressed completely and honestly—not answered, really, but confronted.

And just here is one way that bioregionalism reveals, at least to me, its particular power: for it addresses the how-to-get problem inherently, proffering some practical ideas about strategies, some ways to think about solutions, suggesting not merely an end, I would argue, but a process, not merely a destination but a map.

To make of it more than it deserves would be a mistake, but as near as I can tell it satisfies all the essential conditions of an effective political project, particularly these three: it is irrevocably grounded in historical realities, not just those of the traditional societies that have characterized most of human history but of the American people for most of the last three centuries; it accords well with the apparent patterns of the present, here and elsewhere in the industrial world; and its visions of the future seem practical and real, possible to realize without extraordinary technical or psychological wrenchings of the world as we know it.

Those three conditions will be explored in the pages that follow.

· · ·

The first requirement of a political project is that it stem from actual historical conditions, from the way things have been rather than simply how one would like them to be. Bioregionalism meets this test amply, for as we have already seen it is only the modern version of a perception of the world so ancient it goes back not merely to the early Greeks, who gave it

136

its Gaean form, but to the earliest settled societies known. It has to mean something that so many cultures in so many contexts appreciated this wisdom, and for so many eons lived by it.

But lest that notion seem too rarefied, too tied to the naive and unrecoverable past, let me certify the historical validity of this concept by offering evidence from the more recent past, and the American one at that. As art dealers certify the authenticity of an Old Master by providing its *provenance*, I would suggest the legitimacy of the bioregional idea by examining its roots in the American soil.

Walt Whitman, America's poet, knew us as "a nation of nations," not one people from coast to coast but a different people from state to state and valley to valley. Regionalism has always defined the American experience, and it is by any reckoning as American as—well, as apple, peach, Boston cream, mince, shoofly, bourbon, apricot, date, pecan, or Key lime pie. Whether thought of as sectionalism, localism, separatism, or nullificationism, whether identified with Jeffersonians, Regulators, Agrarians, Grangers, or States-righters—and those are just *some* of the names by which it has gone in our history—regionalism has been recurrent in American life, in its political experience and social patterning as in its speech, food, housing, literature, religion, folk art, and sense of humor.

Out of the great range of scholarly evidence here, I would like to pick four exemplars. That is far too few, but these are giants I am dealing with, people who may be thought of as filling a considerable part of the canvas of 20th-century American scholarship.

Frederick Jackson Turner. Though he became instantly famous and is still remembered for a paper he delivered in 1893, at the very start of his career, on "The Significance of the Frontier in American History," Turner in fact devoted his professional life to a study of what he called, in the paper he wrote at the end of his career in 1924, "The Significance of the Section in American History." And by "section" he meant what he also called a "geographic province" or "geographical region," something very much akin to a bioregion. As he put it:

In every state of the Union there are geographic regions, chiefly, but not exclusively, those determined by the ancient forces of geology, which divide the state into the lesser sections. These subsections within the states often cross state lines and connect with like areas in neighboring states and even in different sections of the larger type. . . . There is, then, a sectionalism of the regions within the larger divisions, a sectionalism of minority areas, sometimes protesting against the policies of the larger section in which they lie and finding more in common with similar regions outside of this section.

For Turner such sections as these provided the only way to understand the patterns of American settlement and migration, of economic and political history, of architecture, literature, and social custom. He saw how different kinds of geography led to different kinds of regional development:

The American people were not passing into a monotonously uniform space. Rather, even in the colonial period, they were entering successive geographic provinces; they were pouring their plastic pioneer life into geographic moulds. They would modify those moulds, they would have progressive revelations of the capacities of the geographic provinces which they won and settled and developed; but even the task of dealing constructively with the different regions would work its effects upon their traits. Not a uniform surface, but a kind of checkerboard of differing environments, lay before them in their settlement.

It was exactly this sort of regional checkerboard that for Turner best explained American political life. As a historian, he saw that disagreements that seemed like random political rivalries and accidental policy disputes were in fact based on geographical rivalries. He concluded:

> A study of votes in the federal House and Senate from the beginning of our national history reveals the fact that party voting has more often broken down than maintained itself on fundamental issues; that when these votes are mapped or tabulated by the congressional districts or states from which those who cast them came, instead of by alphabetical arrangement, a persistent sectional pattern emerges. . . . Legislation is determined less by party than by sectional voting.

Considering the stature of the proponent and the painstaking detail of his substantiation, one would have thought that the "sectional theory," as it was called, would have swept the historical world and become lodged in the popular consciousness. It did not happen that way; the times were uncongenial.

While Europe in the first decades of the century was producing a whole range of scholars bent on examining Europe and the world in terms of regions—notably Vidal de la Blache, Friederich Ratzel, Frédéric Le Play, and Patrick Geddes—scholarship in the United States shied away from anything that would challenge the myths of unity and identity on which American patriotism so heavily depended. And particularly so in that era, when the country, in addition to engaging in two highly jingoistic and xenophobic wars, was going through a period of centralization and national consolidation unlike any it had experienced before—a period in which the national government first asserted its power to tax citizens' income, conscript any and all civilians for the army, establish a national banking system, create a national police force, and control the individual's intake of alcohol.

Hence there was little enthusiasm here for dwelling upon sectional differences underlying presumed national unities, and Turner's work, though it could not be disparaged, was treated with something like embarrassment in much of the historical establishment;* even his own graduate students did not take long to get the message that there were more profitable routes to professional advancement. It was undoubtedly this fairly chilly reception to what he knew in his mind and heart was an unimpeachable concept of signal importance in historical scholarship that kept Turner from producing more than he did. Unlike the majority of his colleagues, he wrote only two books during his lifetime (one of them only a collection of previously published essays), and his *magnum opuses* (*The Significance of Sections in American History* and *The United States 1830–50: The Nation and Its Sections*) were not published until after his death. It is probably not accidental, though, that they were published in quite a different era from the one he had lived through—the early 1930s, when the abject failure of the national system permitted a wide variety of new interpretations of what America was and was to be, and in fact encouraged a new interest in the revitalization of the regions on which economic sustenance was seen after all to depend.

Turner died a depressed and despondent man in 1932. He never learned that in the newly congenial era his *Significance of Sections*, though ill-treated by much of the historical

*A perhaps extreme but revealing reaction was the comment of one professional reviewer in 1922 that it "comes pretty close to treason."

profession, was—largely thanks to a young historian named Allan Nevins—awarded the 1932 Pulitzer Prize for history.

Lewis Mumford. It is hardly a wonder that as brilliant and protean a mind as Mumford's would come to an appreciation of American regionalism, but it is significant that he was not alone.

In the very decade that Turner was feeling most dispirited about his failure to convince America of a need for "the vigorous development of a highly organized provincial life to serve as a check upon mob psychology on a national scale," Mumford was the catalyst of a group in New York (though apparently never known to Turner) formed for just that purpose. It was called the Regional Plan Association of America, and in its brief decade of publishing and advocacy (1923–1933) it established itself as perhaps the most inventive and far-reaching regional organization—and in many respects the most original *planning* organization—this country has ever seen. Its careful and comprehensive work in those years to establish "the region as the basic planning framework," in the words of the British planning expert Frederic J. Osborn, "constitute one of the most important, and still unfinished, chapters in American planning history."

The intellectual foundation for the RPAA's work was laid by Mumford and colleagues in a special issue of *Survey Graphic* magazine in 1925 devoted to the subject, then quite new, of regional planning. A few quotations from Mumford's trenchant piece show clearly how deep is the bioregional heritage and how old the bioregional vision.

Regional planning asks not how wide an area can be brought under the aegis of the metropolis, but how the population and civic facilities can be distributed so as to promote and stimulate a vivid, creative life throughout a whole region—a region being any geographic area that possesses a certain unity of climate, soil, vegetation, industry and culture. The regionalist attempts to plan such an area so that all its sites and resources, from forest to city, from highland to water level, may be soundly developed, and so that the population will be distributed so as to utilize, rather than to nullify or destroy, its natural advantages. It sees people, industry and the land as a single unit.

That, I trust, has a familiar ring to it, and so too this:

Regional planning sees that the depopulated countryside and the congested city are intimately related; it sees that we waste vast quantities of time and energy by ignoring the potential resources of a region, that is, by forgetting all that lies between the terminal points and junctions of our great railroads. Permanent agriculture instead of land-skinning, permanent forestry instead of timber mining, permanent human communities, dedicated to life, liberty and the pursuit of happiness, instead of camps and squatter-settlements, and to stable building, instead of the scantling and falsework of our "go-ahead" communities [i.e., the growing suburbs of the 1920s]—all this is embodied in regional planning.

Mumford's conclusion has a contemporary ring, for indeed it is as true today as it was then:

The technical means of achieving this new distribution of power are at hand. The question before us is whether the automatic operation of physical and financial forces is to burke our rising demand for a more vital and happy kind of existence, or whether, by coordinating our efforts and imaginatively grasping our opportunity, we can remold our institutions so as to promote a regional development—development that will eliminate our enormous economic wastes, give a new life to stable agriculture, set down fresh communities planned on a human scale, and above all, restore a little happiness and freedom in places where these things have been pretty well wrung out. This is a question that cuts diametrically across a large part of our current political and social problems; some of these it places in a new light, and some of them it makes meaningless. Regionalism or super-congestion?

The question, alas, may still be asked sixty years later.

Although the Regional Plan Association disbanded in 1933, believing (mistakenly, as it turned out) that its ideas had been absorbed into the New Deal, Mumford himself never abandoned this regional ideal and in one way or another it shines through all his subsequent masterful works. His perhaps most eloquent statement of it came at the end of that same decade, a time that seemed to him propitious: "The re-animation and re-building of regions, as deliberate works of collective art, is the grand task of politics for the opening generation." As it turned out, of course, that generation was preoccupied with far different tasks and put its energies into the building of national governments everywhere that sought the *de*-animation and destruction of regions. Nevertheless, the Mumfordian vision, as expressed in his *The Culture of Cities* in 1938, remains as reasonable, and vibrant, as ever:

We must create in every region people who will be accustomed, from school onward, to humanist attitudes, co-operative methods, rational controls. These people will know in detail where they live and how they live: they will be united by a common feeling for their landscape, their literature and language, their local ways, and out of their own self-respect they will have a sympathetic understanding with other regions and different local peculiarities. They will be actively interested in the form and culture of their locality, which means their community and their own personalities. Such people will contrib-

143

ute to our land-planning, our industry planning, our community planning the authority of their own understanding, and the pressure of their own desires.

To know in detail where and how one lives is nothing less than the bioregional goal.

Howard Odum. The decade of the 1930s provided a natural seedbed for the ideas of regionalism, and in the academic world they flowered under the attention of a great many professions, from geographers to sociologists, economists to ecologists, historians to anthropologists, architects to literary critics. Of all the scholars drawn to it—people of the stature of Rupert Vance, John Crowe Ransom, Allen Tate, Carl O. Sauer, Robert Park, Stuart Chase, Felix Frankfurter—none was more diligent, none more catholic, than Howard Washington Odum.

Though Odum was a sociologist, the school of regional studies that grew up around him at the University of North Carolina in this decade reflected this whole range of multidisciplinary attention. For nearly two decades he and his colleagues produced a score of books, dozens of research papers and theses, and several hundred scholarly articles (fifty-nine of them in Odum's own quarterly, *Social Forces*), all to the point of showing that regionalism "may be the key to a better understanding of the past," in Odum's words, "and the richer development of the future, to the theoretical study of our society, and to the practical planning of its new frontiers." The centerpiece of all that effort was his massive 1938 study, with Harry Estill Moore, *American Regionalism.*

Odum was, alas, a terrible writer, squarely within the American sociological tradition, and some of the effect of that volume must have been blunted by its verbosity. It was nonetheless rigorous and comprehensive, touching on all the social sciences, and it showed how much regional work was being done in the country and how essential the regional understanding was for further academic work and for the reconstruction of post-Depression America.

Like Turner and Mumford, Odum began with the environment:

> Whatever else regionalism may or may not be, its first essence is to be found in the geographic factor. The mudsill of the idea of regionalism is that social phenomena may best be understood when considered in relation to the area in which they occur as a cultural frame of reference. . . . To some regionalists this means that social phenomena are determined by the purely physical facts of nature such as geology, topography, climate; to others it means that physical environment and the expression of those physical facts in vegetation, animal life, changes of the face of nature affected by man, etc., make possible certain adaptations which man may or may not make in accordance with other factors such as culture.

Odum then went on to examine as many of those "factors" as he could, and his demonstration of the extent and complexity of regionalism in America is probably unsurpassable. He cited the geographers' 700 soil regions and 514 agricultural regions, the ecologists' 17 watersheds and 97 river valleys, the city planners' 183 metropolitan regions and 683 retail-shopping regions, the anthropologists' American Indian "culture areas," the historians' sections and provinces, the political scientists' pluralisms and federalisms, and the literary critics' cultures in the South, Southwest, New England, and the Great Plains. But it was the economists' work, naturally, given the times, that interested him most and where his analysis is most compelling:

> Regionalism . . . represents the philosophy and technique of self-help, self-development, and initiative in which each areal unit is not only aided, but is committed to the fuller develop-

ment of its own resources and capacities. It assumes that the key to the redistribution of wealth and the equalization of opportunity will be found in the capacity of each region to create wealth and, through new reaches of consumption of commodities, maintain the capacity and retain that wealth in well-balanced production and consumption programs.

Regionalism is thus essentially an economy not of scarcity but of abundance, to the end that all the people may have access to adequate food, clothing, housing, tools, occupational opportunity—an accomplishment to be made possible through regional techniques of use as well as production.

American Regionalism is an important piece of scholarship and irrefutable proof of an American reality. But though it had its vogue, and though Odum went on for another decade advancing its cause, the concept of regionalism did not make much headway in the two decades of extreme centralization that followed the 1930s. Odum's journal, *Social Forces*, which had been full of regional studies under his tutelage, printed only five during the 1950s and, by the 1960s, none.

National Resources Committee. It was in this same fruitful Depression decade that even the Federal government got into the thicket of regionalism and, surprisingly, emerged with a body of elaborate studies proving that, indeed, America could be understood only as "a nation of nations."

In its central document, *Regional Factors in National Planning and Development*, issued in 1935, the committee was quite forthright:

Regional differentiation . . . may turn out to be the true expression of American life and culture . . . [reflecting] American ideals, needs, and viewpoints far more adequately than does State consciousness and loyalty. One might conclude, therefore, that it should not only be conserved but augmented and utilized as a major factor in national planning and development.

That's quite a mouthful—indeed, for Washington, quite a confession. From it stems the inevitable idea that at least some of the processes of government should be decentralized to the region:

> Development, in reality the whole program of government, emerges not only from State and national attitudes and desires, but very importantly also from needs and purposes which can only be described as "regional," from "regional consciousness" and "regional climates of opinion."

The report naturally includes required disclaimers about how far regional government should go: "The 'regionalism' here discussed is not a Balkanization of the United States" or "a new form of sovereignty" with "elected officers, a legislative body and the power to tax." But more than once it is forced by its own logic to recommend something close to that. It castigates "the overconcentration of decisions at the center" and indicates that decentralization of decision-making and "the very stimulation of the self-consciousness of the section" would ultimately provide "a wider leadership for civic affairs." And it recognizes that the basic troubles of the country simply cannot be handled by the Federal government or even by the states: "The problems to be treated do not follow State lines but resolve themselves into regional units, and hence do not often lend themselves to treatment by existing political arrangements."

In the end, the report even admits that natural resources are essentially regional and that the economic problems of the nation can best be solved by recognizing that fact. And, almost astonishingly, it wonders aloud what might be the future for regions in control of their own resources: "Should such re-

gions seek specialization based upon their peculiarities of resources to form an organic whole as a nation, or should they
seek autonomous self-containment?"

Clearly those were heady days in Washington, so it is not
surprising that the report ends on a remarkably rosy note:
"Regionalism," it confidently argues, "has made enormous
strides in recent years. It is a movement which may be expected to progress steadily and rapidly."

. . .

That it did not, of course, has to do with the vagaries of history
and the deliberate policies of those to whom the decentralization of power is threatening. Instead it was forced to wait
through the long decades of what was tried out as "the American century," only gradually asserting itself as the failures of
the mammoth state and its industrial monoculture began to
make themselves manifest.

The regional impulse did not disappear, to be sure; it is
much too grounded for that. There were significant traces all
through the 1950s and '60s: Merrill Jensen's important scholarly compendium, *Regionalism in America*, came out in 1951
(with a foreword by Felix Frankfurter: "Regionalism is a recognition of the intractable diversities among men"), a Regional Science Association was formed in 1954, comparative
state and regional political analysis blossomed in the late '50s
and early '60s, regional planning became a fixed academic discipline in the '60s, the Federal government established its
Area Development and Regional Action commissions from
1961 on, and Ian McHarg's groundbreaking *Design With Nature* was published in 1969, and that is merely skimming over
the highlights. But it was not until more recently still that
regionalism was to enjoy a true renaissance.

Bioregionalism, then, is hardly a new concept; it is, rather, a contemporary expression of a very old and many-sided one. That gives its adherents something that almost no other movement around of any kind can give: the knowledge that they are rooted in a tradition long known and long cherished in this country, that theirs is a provenance of validity and authority.

TEN

Present Currents

THOUGH occasionally a political movement achieves success by apparently going against the dominant currents of its time and culture, in fact almost always such movements operate—even if their adherents do not always realize it—in accordance with the deepest and longest-running tides of their society.

The mobilization of the Indian citizenry against the Raj must have seemed in most ways a bizarre enterprise when Gandhi began it in the 1930s, and certainly many colonial officers and not a few Indian satraps would have said it was a totally misguided attempt to deny the historical inevitability of British colonialism. Yet it not only responded to a real and powerful, if latent, desire on the part of most Indians for independence and autonomy, it was also very much a part of a visible worldwide trend toward the assertion of ethnic rights and national aspirations.

Similarly, the civil rights movement in this country must have seemed to many, even many who joined it, a brave but futile effort when it began in 1960, ranged as it was against decades of entrenched custom and power in the South and against elaborate patterns of racist acquiescence in the entire society. Yet the movement was quite consistent with the abiding (at least professed) American values of equality and justice and the growing racial guilt they had produced in the years since World War II, and was quite of a piece with the declarations of racial power and pride being enunciated throughout the world just then from independent Ghana to revolutionary Vietnam.

A political current cannot run against the tide of its society, not successfully, not long: if it tries, it can at best create a temporary backwash, roiling the waters in a brief gyration of contrariety, or become contained in harmless eddies continually going around in circles at the edges. It can deviate from the mainstream, to be sure, and it can run its own course and even make its own channels, but it cannot reverse or deny the flow and current in which it lives. That is why most revolutions fail, and those that seem to succeed are still every bit a part of the society that spawned them, some only creating more of what they have presumed to dispel—the Bourbon Napoleon, the Czar Stalin, the Emperor Mao.

. . .

The political project of bioregionalism, as must be clear by now, has promise precisely because it conforms so well with so many of the underlying trends of the contemporary world, particularly the American part. It stands against a good deal of the current mythology, that is true: against pollution in the name of jobs, nuclear terror in the name of security, growth in the name of economy, destruction in the name of progress, despoliation in the name of profits. But it is, in sinew and blood, thoroughly expressive of the basic trends of the late 20th century, and its vision is far more attuned to current realities and natural imperatives than, say, those of Adam Smith or Alexander Hamilton or Andrew Carnegie, in whose names we continue so much errancy today.

Bioregionalism is, for a start, an obvious manifestation of the deep worldwide concern for the environment that has affected practically every private citizen and every public policy around the globe since the Stockholm conference just over a decade ago.

It is grounded in and in a sense takes inspiration from the worldwide feminist upsurge of the last few decades, expressing those traits of nurturance, holism, communality, and spirituality that have marked the philosophy of the women's movement.

It shares the profound distrust of bigness, of centralized government, and of arbitrary authority that have surfaced in all developed and most developing nations in recent years, and joins with that broad and still inchoate movement in most industrial nations toward what has variously been called "backyard democracy," "grassroots politics," "citizen empowerment," or "community control."

Above all, bioregionalism is a natural and organic response to what is arguably the most profound contemporary trend of all: the disintegration of the established forms and systems that have characterized the Western world—its industrial economy, its mass society, its nation-state—for most of the last five centuries. Elsewhere I have assembled some of the voices in the chorus of scholars who are agreed on the fact (if not the consequences) of this trend, but suffice it here to say that they range through all academic disciplines from physics to philosophy, and through all political persuasions from anarchist to authoritarian. Whether this disintegration foretells an "oncoming age of scarcity" (the Club of Rome) or the "twilight of authority" (Robert Nisbet) or "the end of the American era" (Andrew Hacker) or "the coming dark ages" (L. S. Stavrianos), it does seem to be leading us inexorably toward some kind of shakedown in the ways of ordering power, a search for some more creative and responsive political and economic institutions, for which the bioregional vision seems especially appropriate.

But there is still one more singular, and singularly apposite, way in which the bioregional message is consistent with the tenor of its age. Because it serves better than anything else to suggest not only the appropriateness but the ultimate validity for our time of the bioregional idea, I would like to examine it in some detail, in both its global and its American contexts.

. . .

I have already mentioned that a few years back political scientist Harold Isaacs perceived that the characteristic political phenomenon of the postwar era is "the world breaking into its bits and pieces." He goes on to say, and throughout his book, *Idols of the Tribe*, to prove:

> This great shaking out of all power and group relations is global in extent. It has come about as a result of the collapse or weakening of power systems or larger coherences that for periods of time managed to hold their clusters of separate groups under the control of a single dominant group or coalition of groups.

It is, in his nice word, a "fragmentation" of old political forms and allegiances, and the evidence for it, the telling shards as it were, are to be found everywhere.

Indeed, despite the enormous sums and energies spent on propping up old imperial arrangements and continental alliances and a pretended worldwide organization, what we see when we look at the last forty years of world history is a movement not toward larger and more consolidated arrangements but rather toward smaller, more distended, more segmentary ones. At the time of its founding in 1945 the United Nations claimed 51 nations; in 1985 it has 159, and that does not include a dozen sovereign states that are not members. In 1945 there were six acknowledged empires across the globe; today there are none, and the two unacknowledged ones—the American and Russian—have been severely weakened and disjointed, both fighting bloody wars to preserve what remains of their hegemony.

But there is an even more profound process at work along these same lines, less often noticed but every bit as powerful. It is the breakdown of the nation-state itself, the drive *within* the multiplying nations for increased power and self-management, in some cases autonomy and independence, by their constituent parts, the movement that in one form is manifested as *separatism*, in another as *regionalism*.

· · ·

Eric Hobsbawm, the British historian, has called *separatism* "the characteristic nationalist movement of our time" and "an unquestionably active, growing and powerful socio-political force." It is to be found everywhere in the world, on every settled continent, and in one way or another within every state, and it exhibits a pervasiveness and tenacity that not even the sweep of nationalism itself in the 19th century could match. One is tempted to say that it reflects a fundamental human pattern of existence that even the modern nation-state, with all its might and sophistication, has been unable to eradicate.

An exhaustive catalogue of the identifiable separatist movements around the globe would be tedious, so numerous are they. Louis L. Snyder's comprehensive *Global Mini-Nationalisms: Autonomy or Independence* lists twenty-nine nations with fifty-eight separatist strains and still fails to mention at least twenty other nations with forty-five other separatist groups and resistant minorities—and that is counting only the most vociferous and self-conscious movements, not even such identifiable but not explicitly antagonistic subpopulations as the Andalusians in Spain, the Ladakhis in India, or the Mohawks in the United States.

Some idea of the extent of the separatist phenomenon can be gained by just a cursory look at only the most active movements in Europe, where, after all, we should expect to find the oldest, strongest, and most cohesive nations in the world. There, on the continent that began and developed the whole national system in the first place, one can distinguish some thirty-six explicit separatist movements: in Britain (Scots, Welsh, Manx, Cornish, Shetlands); France (Alsatians, Bretons, Corsicans, Occitanians); Belgium (Flemings, Walloons); Holland (Fresians); Scandinavia (Lapps, Fresians, Scanias); Germany (Bavarians, Hessians); Switzerland (Jurassics); Spain (Basques, Catalans, Canary Islanders); Italy (Sicilians, Tyroleans); Yugoslavia (Croats, Bosnians, Macedonians, Montenegrins, Serbs); Rumania (Germans); USSR (Latvians, Lithuanians, Estonians, Armenians, Azerbaijanis, Ukrainians, Georgians, not counting Asian separatists).

In other words, quite surprising evidence of the persistence of the separatist spirit on this theoretically cohesive territory. And not because there is any outside force at work—no communist conspiracy, no capitalist plot, no foreign pressure—but because it is rooted in the centuries-old historical reality of the continent.

European separatism—separatism anywhere—is not exactly bioregionalism, of course, and, except for small groups in West Germany and Britain and several Indian tribes in this country, none of the separatist movements has allied itself with ecological politics in any explicit way. But virtually all the ethnic, religious, or tribal differences that give rise to it are rooted in geographical differences as well, and many of the groups in specifying their homeland demarcate what clearly can be regarded as a bioregion, most often something like a georegion. This is particularly easy to see in places like Wales, Corsica, Jura, or Catalonia, where the ethnic region is virtually identical with an obvious geographic feature, but it is no less true of Brittany, Alsace, or Croatia—or for that matter Baluchistan, Kashmir, Sarawak, Eritrea, Quebec, or Dinē (Navajo-land).

No special mystery to that, really. The movements stem from people long associated with the land and connected to regional histories going back many centuries, and the special character of that land has given them those special differences of language and dress and music and folklore that they now strive to preserve. It is precisely because they are so connected to their geography, in fact, that these peoples have lasted so long as separate entities with separate cultures, despite the considerable efforts of their national governments to eradicate their languages, destroy their institutions, and deny their heritages.

Not only have they survived, but in most places today their movements are growing stronger and winning more and more battles for recognition and autonomy. Michael Zwerin, a journalist who spent many years exploring the separatist movements of Europe, came to this conclusion: "The pendulum which for centuries has been swinging towards larger political groupings is swinging back and just as exterior colonies broke away from empires to form the Third World, so internal colonies—the Fourth World—are now trying to break away from States."

. . .

The other and usually less militant form of the fragmentary process is *regionalism*, and it too has been growing with special force over these past several decades.

Regionalism—the conscious breaking down of larger national structures into smaller and more manageable ones, and the self-conscious perception of differences of place—is not the same order of political and cultural force as separatism, and it seldom has the same kind of drive toward autonomy. Indeed, insofar as it does not threaten any overall national hegemony, it is often welcomed and in some cases even fostered by the national government, usually as a merely practical means of governance, a way to deliver services in countries grown otherwise too big and inefficient. But it stems from the same felt needs as separatism does and is every bit as important a response to the currents of the era.

Regionalism is without question a worldwide phenomenon—it is, according to English regional specialist Hugh Clout, "in the forefront of the international political arena"—but it is strongest in those states where sheer size and numbers prevent effective centralization, and that is as true of rigid and hierarchical societies like those of China and Russia as it is of more open ones like those of India, Brazil, Canada, and the United States. China has worked for some years to accommodate (and keep under control) its numerous regional minorities, with whole ministries and elaborate campaigns devoted to the tasks, and Russia has been forced in the last decade to allow increased autonomy and both language and cultural rights to various of its separate republics as a way to try to stem regional passions. In India, only a pastiche of more than two dozen regions to begin with, regional tensions have recently come to an all-time high—the Punjabi autonomy movement, temporarily checked through brutal army onslaughts in 1984, being the most notable; even the ruling parties there have been forced to give up on the fiction of national uniformity: "Regional consciousness," says the senior Janata Party parliamentarian, Syed Shahabuddin, "will be the main

struggle in the next decade, to set up a new equilibrium between the center, the states, and the grassroots." In Canada,
quite apart from the still-potent movement for Quebec separatism, the whole question of increasing provincial power and
soothing regional passions has dominated the political agenda
of the last half-dozen years and is likely to do so for the foreseeable future.

Naturally the academic and bureaucratic response to regional power has been to develop a whole new discipline, regional development and planning. It has now become a fixed
part of the governments of virtually all industrial and a good
many developing nations, as well as such supranational organizations as the World Bank and the European Economic
Commission; the last has had an explicit policy on regional
development since 1972, and its Common Regional Fund
spent nearly two million pounds between 1975 and 1980. Specialized regional study institutes and university departments,
complete with their own range of textbooks, specialized journals, and international conferences, have been created in more
than twenty-five countries in all parts of the world.

In this country the centrifugal pulls of regionalism, despite
all the efforts impelling national unity and patriotism, have
never been stronger than in the last dozen years. "The Balkanization of nations is a worldwide phenomenon," economist
Lester Thurow noted in 1980, "that the United States has not
escaped." That same word—"Balkanization," a disparaging
reference to what was actually a pretty sensible system of recognizing the ethnic disparities of southern Europe—has also
been used by many other observers, from former cabinet of-
ficer James Schlesinger on the liberal side to writer Kevin Phil-
lips on the conservative, and any number of commentators
have remarked on the same process.

A decade ago *Business Week* noted the emergence of a new

"civil war between the states"; a Washington research group, Editorial Research Reports, issued a pamphlet on the "Resurgence of Regionalism" in 1977; the *National Journal* had a lengthy series on "the rise of regionalism" in 1976 and then again, reaffirming the trends, in 1983; *Congressional Quarterly* in a special article in 1980 said, "It is beyond argument that regionalism remains strong in the U.S.—and for good and proper reasons." In a long study of "regional diversity" in 1981, the Harvard-MIT Joint Center for Urban Studies noted that although "political conflict among regions . . . has always been important in the United States," it has "moved away from accommodation toward confrontation in recent years," especially in the economic realm: there are "emerging economic differences among the regions" and "sharp differences in regional growth rates," and these trends "will continue for some time." Ann Markusen, a regional planner at Cornell, found that "the new regionalism" was a "prominent feature of modern political life" and pointed to "the emergence in the 1970s in academia, in the lobbying world, in regional organizations, and in the state itself (especially Congress) of a strong regional identification and assertion of conflicting interests."

But perhaps Dana Fradon's *New Yorker* cartoon said this best. It showed a man at a bar, his glass raised high, proclaiming: "My section of the country, right or wrong."

The regional resurgence, which shows no signs of abating, has manifested itself in all sorts of ways. *The Wall Street Journal* began a weekly column of American regional reports in 1982, and *The New York Times* started its regular feature of "Regional Notebook" from different sections of the country in 1984. The long-awaited *Dictionary of American Regional English* was scheduled to be published in 1985, confirming sharp regional variations in culture and language. Regional rivalries have given rise to such groups as the Midwest Institute, the New England Council, the Southern Growth Policies Board, and the Western Governors Policy Office, and these political bodies have been mirrored by similar caucuses in Congress. Newspapers and magazines regularly feature the "new" American regional cooking, part of what *Cuisine* magazine has described as America "in the throes of rediscovering its regional cuisines." There are regional theaters (150 principal groups), regional dance companies (400), regional television and film organizations, and, in literature, what critic Robert Towers has called the emergence of "the New Regionalists."

Such a sweeping wave has not missed the universities, either. After a long period of uninterest, geographers began re-examining American regions in the 1970s, and one academic reported then that "the regional concept—which holds that the face of the earth can be marked off into areas of distinctive character—constitutes the core of geography." Economists, who had begun to develop a regional *science* in the 1950s (a discipline that now boasts nineteen journals and fourteen degree-granting universities), broadened out to create programs in regional *economics* (what one economist calls "what is where, and why, and so what?") and regional *development* in every serious economics department in the country. Regional planning, which had been a marginal and lagging discipline until the 1960s, suddenly took on a whole new life; the number of planners expanded exponentially (today there are 16,000 professionals), and now there are nine academic journals, annual academic meetings, and more than sixty graduate planning departments. Regional concepts in recent years have even become a fixed part of such disciplines as anthropology, sociology, archeology, and political science.

And, naturally, regionalism has also taken governmental

shape. Regional planning and development has been a Federal concern since the 1930s, as we saw, with the Tennessee Valley Authority its ongoing manifestation from 1933, but not until the 1960s was a concerted effort made to promote regional development nationwide. An Area Development Administration was created in 1961 and in 1965 that was expanded into the Economic Development Administration, which created the Appalachian Regional Commission, the first regional authority since the TVA, and subsequently eleven other "Title V" regional commissions and 1,729 smaller planning areas. In 1969 the Office of Management and the Budget issued its "A-95" regulation creating regional planning and development clearinghouses across the nation, and this program has subsequently expanded to an establishment of almost 600 regional councils, 488 substate planning districts, and at the last count 1,932 regional organizations to plan and carry out Federally funded services.

. . .

Regionalism has enjoyed this remarkable renaissance for a great many reasons—economic rivalries in an era of economic stagnation, new environmental and therefore geographic concerns, growing scarcities of regional resources, the growth of the service (and inevitably location-based) economy, regional competition for Federal allocations, population growth and mobility—but no cause is so fundamental as that the national government has simply proved itself inadequate. Increasingly through the 1960s and '70s, Washington showed beyond peradventure that it could not solve the mounting problems of the society, could not even properly analyze them at a national scale, and all the promises it had made and money it had dispensed in an effort to do so were generally seen as inefficient—

and both Carter and Reagan came to office on the strength of the reaction against this failed liberalism.

Increasingly, too, and complementarily, it became clear that most of the serious ills of the age, from air pollution to commuter traffic congestion, were actually regional in scope, and neither the national nor state governments on the one hand nor the municipal governments on the other were really able to confront them efficiently. This realization has accounted for the explosive increase in the number of "special district governments"—regional agencies that transcend city and state boundaries to handle problems of water, sanitation, energy, transportation, and the like—from 18,000 in the 1960s to nearly 30,000 today.

Regionalism, in short, seems to have grown in this last decade primarily as a natural response to perceived inadequacies, a resurfacing of the underlying geographic realities that had been there all along, a reaffirmation of those old perceptions of Turner and Mumford and the rest that America *is* its regions. That this resurgence has happened without much coherence, with poorly understood motives and poorly planned organizations, and with no great understanding by the public at large of its character, does not mean that it is any less appropriate a response, any less significant a demonstration of the true nature of the society. Rather, it suggests that the real need now is to take it all one step—or several steps—further and develop our regional consciousnesses and cultures and institutions with an explicit sense of purpose, making self-conscious and conspicuous what so far has been largely ignored or only dimly understood.

Which is exactly what bioregionalism allows us, and why it is so appropriately a movement of its time.

ELEVEN

Future Visions

IT MIGHT AT FIRST seem curious, or typically perverse, for George Bernard Shaw to have chosen the Serpent in the Garden as the enunciator of those famous words, "Some men see things as they are and say *Why?* Others dream things that never were and say *Why not?*" Could Shaw have really thought there was something satanic in that profound question, *Why not?*, or was he perhaps suggesting that it is precisely the most *human* question of all, the one surest to appeal to Eve and for Eve to use on Adam? For it springs from that eternal restless quest for development, enrichment, and refinement, that need to extend visions and capabilities and lives, that has characterized the human animal from its remotest beginnings. Dreaming things that never were may be the occupation of fools and visionaries, but it can be said that we are, all things considered, better off today because Columbus dreamed of finding India and Pasteur of killing bacteria, because the people of Salzburg dreamed of a cathedral and those of Cordoba a university, because the Athenians dreamed of democracy, the Founding Fathers of federalism, because Mozart dreamed of a forty-first symphony, Melville of a white whale, Michelangelo of the finger of his God.

So, too, bioregionalism can be accused of dreaming things that never were, at least never in the range and sophistication I have been suggesting in these pages. No ancient Greeks, no pre-Columbian Indians, no hunter-gatherer societies, however they may have lived by Gaean precepts, ever had the kind of ecological understanding we now have, or the philosophies of the world to choose from that we now do, or the extent of tools and measurements and techniques of knowing the earth that we now command. And yet, as must be obvious by now, bioregionalism dreams things that are not so fantastic, so incomprehensible, so other-worldly at all; it does not demand a world of Walden IIs or Erewhons, it does not posit a species grown superhuman with enlarged brains, or hearts.

Yes, in a sense it could be regarded, simply by the sweep of its vision, as falling into that category that the dreamless so easily dismiss as "utopian." But a utopia is only a design for a time to come, tomorrow-in-genesis, the present articulation of the possible future; and bioregionalism is only a way to begin to imagine, design, and create that future as soon as possible. As the philosopher Leszek Kolakowski has so neatly put it: "It may well be that the impossible at a given moment can become possible only by being stated at a time when it is impossible."

It is exactly because the bioregional dreams do not do violence to eternal truths—and in fact *express* human and biotic truths—that they can commend themselves as the final reason for regarding bioregionalism as an effective political project. It is, however distant a reality we may regard it now, a perfectly plausible future, and the vision has the undoubted air of the practical, the do-able, the achievable. Let me elaborate.

· · ·

For one thing, the basic idea of a region is after all a matter of common consciousness and parlance: people do, in fact, think of themselves as inhabiting regions, even if not precisely bioregions. Kevin Lynch, the brilliant urban planner at MIT, concluded after a study on *Managing the Sense of a Region*, "Our senses are local, while our experience is regional," and he produced twenty-three studies of regional attitudes to back him up. One, by a sociologist who saturated the country with postcards to newspapers, bureaucrats, and county officials, discovered that people in this country see themselves as inhabiting no fewer than 295 regions, ranging from the obvious weathervane North-East-South-West down to Sacramento Valley and Little Dixie and Lowlands and Finger Lakes and Boonslick.

The extension of that natural perception into a biotic perception is, I have discovered, not very hard to make: people are fairly savvy about the places they live in if you give them a little time to think about it. Ask them about their watersheds, whether they set out tomatoes on May Day, and if they are used to seeing coyotes or German roaches or deer by the road, and you will get a pretty good idea of their regional understanding. Lee Swenson, one of the early bioregionalists, took a bioregional seminar across the country a few years ago and reported that it might take an hour or two, sometimes a full morning, but he never failed to get his audience, no matter how mixed, to come up with a consensus about the contours of the region they lived in that matched in remarkable detail the ecological definition of their bioregion. In some way, people tend to comprehend—even though they are seldom taught about—the spaces they inhabit.

People also know that their region's environment is being assaulted and imperiled, most often by forces they do not understand and cannot control. The notion of environmental health is quite new in the public consciousness, but today—thanks, alas, to toxic wastes seeping into schoolyards, chemical spills forcing the evacuation of towns, smog "alerts" making people stay indoors, poison runoffs leading to undrinkable groundwater, acid rains killing fish in mountain ponds—it is always one of those issues the public opinion polls, as in the 1984 elections, show to be at the very top of American concerns. Helplessness in the face of environmental crises has been the usual response to date, since there are no public or private institutions yet geared to do anything serious and drastic about it, but experience has shown—in the cases of Love Canal, for example, the Clearwater project on the Hudson, and toxic-waste laws in New Jersey—that the public can be aroused and politically energized on these issues.

These basic understandings, then, allow the bioregional project a set of tools that other more arcane political programs may not have. Since the task is to get people to know their bioregion and the threats to it, organizers can enlist high school science classes to examine the local river and survey its biota, local conservation groups to do a survey of the region's trees, community college students to study local waste-disposal systems and agricultural runoffs, university economics majors to try an input-output analysis of regional goods and services. The possibilities are endless—there is after all a well-established science of chorography, the study of regions—and information about how to conduct ecological studies and resource surveys is easily obtainable.

The sum of all these efforts might be assembled and then distributed throughout the region, perhaps in the form of a "bundle" describing the configuration and resources of the region, where it is healthy and where it is strained. The bundle—a concept borrowed from American Indian tribes—has been used for several years now by people in the bioregional movement as a way of learning about the nature of the places they inhabit, and then of teaching other groups and organizing projects for the region. Typically a bundle will have a map of the bioregion, a description of the types of trees and flowers, mammals and birds, and insects and fishes that are common to it, a few items on its history and earliest occupants, a drawing and a poem or two, and perhaps a list of current groups working on ecological, communitarian, or bioregional projects. But it can be anything, depending on the nature of the region and the depth of commitment, and it can of course be organic, growing year by year as the analyses continue and concerns multiply.

. . .

The second reason bioregionalism seems achievable is that, because its concepts are so basically accessible, it can aim at people beyond the usual constituencies for social change. Not that those constituencies are insubstantial—they amount, by various estimates, to somewhere between 5 million and 10 million people—but they do not by themselves constitute a movement sufficient for the broad and thoroughgoing reshaping of this country that is necessary.

The bioregional idea has the potential to join what are traditionally thought of as Right and Left in America because it is built upon and appeals to values that, at bottom, are shared by those who identify with those two tendencies.* They have

*It is Michael Marien's shrewd perception that politics should be seen not in terms of a flat earth, where Left and Right are represented at the extremes and are never thought of as congruent, but rather of a round earth, where the authoritarian Left (e.g., Stalinism) and the authoritarian Right (e.g., Nazism), having so much in common, overlap with each other at the top, and the libertarian Right (e.g., American "Lib-

in common, for example, a belief in local control, self-reliance, town-meeting democracy, community power, and decentralism, all basic elements in what are thought of as the traditional American—at least Jeffersonian—values. They both also have a profound (or at least commonly voiced) distrust of distant and arbitrary authority and control, whether exerted by government, public utilities or corporations, and resistance to imposed codes and regulations, restrictive and protective laws, and the siphon of taxes on the individual purse. They commonly share a concern for the natural world, for the wilderness and its species, and usually have some firsthand experience with nature in the raw, whether from deer-hunting or backpacking. And at some level they agree on an underlying appreciation for the rich potential of individualism—this is as fundamental in the American psyche as "all men are created equal"—and on the notion that everyone is capable of making a living, everyone should contribute to the community, everyone can participate in the turmoils of life.

All those ideas are one way or another inherent in bioregionalism and make it capable of uniting many different kinds of people: the National Rifle Association hunter in Pennsylvania with the environmentalist in Colorado, both of whom understand the balances of nature; the woman in the Virginia commune and the housewife on the Iowa farm, both of whom appreciate the importance of self-reliance and therefore of neighborliness; the activist in Vermont who has been fighting a nuclear plant and the farmer in Minnesota who has been

---

ertarianism") and the libertarian Left (e.g., anarchism) share common ground at the bottom. (And wishy-washy liberalism of all kinds spreads across the equator.) In that view, bioregionalism seems to me to be able to occupy a considerable part of the southern hemisphere, from the equivalent of the Tropic of Capricorn on down.

resisting an electric power line on his land, both of whom know the unfeeling power of public bodies that the public doesn't really control. In fact bioregionalism has the potential to blunt and diminish all those other political differences that are made so much of—Republican and Democrat, liberal and conservative—until they seem quite unimportant.

. . .

The bioregional project also takes force from the fact that it can be begun locally, with just a few people willing to study a little, talk a little, imagine a little, organize a little. As its perceptions are regional, so is its canvas, and thus the energies for its launching do not have to be very exhaustive and the resources to keep it moving do not have to be very extensive.

All too many contemporary political schemes try to take aim at the national government—running people for Congress, or nominating one of their own for the Presidency, or creating caucuses in a national party, or setting up lobbies in Washington, or organizing constituencies on a national scale. The efforts are not always useless, but they are far more often symbolic than substantive, and they always entail a great expenditure of money and energy for no very certain or enduring return. Or worse: they discover that it is impossible finally to change the entrenched Federal bureaucracy or the unresponsive Federal administration, and end up teaching people to believe that political action of any kind is inevitably futile.

What makes the bioregional effort different—in any foreseeable future, anyway—is that it asks nothing of the Federal government and needs no national legislation, no governmental regulation, no Presidential dispensation. What commends it especially to its age is that it does not need any Federal presence to promote it, only a Federal obliviousness to permit it.

In that respect it is very much in tune with that basic American spirit once described by Thoreau:

> The government never of itself furthered any enterprise, but by the alacrity with which it got out of the way. *It* does not keep the country free. *It* does not settle the West. *It* does not educate. The character inherent in the American people has done all that has been accomplished; and it would have done somewhat more, if the government had not sometimes got in its way.

Nor, ultimately, unlike various other political movements, does bioregionalism envision a takeover of the national government or a vast rearrangement of the national machinery—nothing so complex, elaborate, uprooting, and frustrating as that. No, its spirit is local and its attentions regional, and it regards questions of national scope to be, at least at this point, genuinely irrelevant. The task, after all, is to build power at the bottom, not to take it away from the top; to release the energies, the long-hidden and systematically blunted energies, of people where they actually live and on the issues they regularly face, not to try to steal the energies, if such were possible, of institutions made unresponsive by their distance and ineffective by their ignorance.

Take care of the pennies and the pounds will take care of themselves. Take care of the communities, develop in regions, tap the local manifestations of "the character inherent in the American people," and the Federal structure can become quite irrelevant.

· · ·

The practicality of the bioregional project is also enhanced by the considerable virtue of already having something of a movement—still nascent, still uncertain of just where and how to go, but with enough staying power to have lasted more than a decade now and to have spread to every corner of the continent.

There are more than sixty self-consciously bioregional groups at present, representing a broad range of talents, interests, and activities.* Some, such as the Ozarks Area Community Congress, hold annual meetings to pass platforms and resolutions on specific areal problems; some, such as the Institute for Social Ecology in Vermont, concentrate on educating people through conferences and seminars; some, such as the San Antonio BioregionalResearch Group and the Siskiyou Regional Education Project, make ecological inventories and promote public awareness of bioregionalism; some, such as Friends of the Trees in Washington state and the National Water Center in Arkansas, as their names imply, have specialized environmental interests; some, such as Max's Pot in Texas and the New Alchemy Institute on Cape Cod, concentrate on developing bioregional technologies; and some, such as the Driftless Bioregional Network in Wisconsin and the Katuah Bioregional Council in the Appalachians, build networks among local organizations concerned with ecological issues.

The bioregional library already established is impressive. Planet Drum has published a half-dozen books and pamphlets as well as bundles from the Rockies, the Northwest, the Hudson Valley, and elsewhere. Fourteen regional magazines are published with some regularity, ranging from *RAIN* in Portland (which has also published a book of bioregional analysis for the Portland area), *TILTH* in Seattle, and *Raise the Stakes* in San Francisco, all of which have been going on for more

*One list is available from Planet Drum, Box 31251, San Francisco, CA 94131.

than a decade, to *Konza* in Kansas and the *Annals of Earth Stewardship* in Massachusetts, now in their second years. And there are probably several dozen books on issues that are more or less specifically bioregional, written by such adherents of the movement as Raymond Dasmann, Gary Snyder, Peter Berg, Murray Bookchin, Morris Berman, Jerry Mander, Gary Coates, Gary Nabhan, Jim Dodge, John and Nancy Todd, Michael Helm, and Donald Worster. (I am not talking about the literally hundreds of other books that speak directly to bioregional concerns by such people as Schumacher, Lovins, Roszak, Capra, Berry, Dubos, Mumford, Kohr, Illich, and Lappé.) All of which adds up to a considerable body of literature on the whats and whys of bioregionalism, on the how-tos and where-to-finds, that few such fledgling movements could boast of.

In just the last two years the movement has felt secure enough in its sense of purpose finally to have spawned a continent-wide organization, the North American Bioregional Congress,* and that in turn has created an initial proto-platform of the bioregional movement—not a definitive sort of document, it is understood, but something like a set of talking-papers to suggest the way bioregionalists have been thinking to date. The preamble may fairly suggest the tone:

Welcome Home

A growing number of people are recognizing that in order to secure the clean air, water and food that we need to healthfully survive, we have to become stewards of the places where we live. People sense the loss in not knowing our neighbors and natural surroundings, and are discovering that the best way to take care of ourselves, and to get to know our neighbors, is to protect and restore where we live.

---

*Later, the Turtle Island Bioregional Gathering.

Bioregionalism recognizes, nurtures, sustains and cele-brates our local connections with: land; plants and animals; rivers, lakes and oceans; air; families, friends and neighbors; community; native traditions; and systems of production and trade.

It is taking the time to learn the possibilities of place.

It is a mindfulness of local environment, history and com-munity aspirations that can lead to a future of safe and sus-tainable life.

It is reliance on well-understood and widely-used sources of food, power and waste disposal.

It is secure employment based on supplying a rich diversity of services within the community and prudent surpluses to other regions.

Bioregionalism is working to satisfy basic needs through local control in schools, health centers, and governments.

The bioregional movement seeks to re-create a widely-shared sense of regional identity founded upon a renewed crit-ical awareness of and respect for the integrity of our natural ecological communities.

People can join with neighbors to discuss ways we can work together to 1) learn what our special local resources *are*, 2) plan how to best protect and use those natural and cultural re-sources, 3) exchange our time and energy to best meet our daily and long-term needs, and 4) enrich our children's local and global knowledge.

Bioregionalism begins by acting responsibly at home. Wel-come home!

What has most impressed me about these people is not only their intelligence but their sense that their own personal bio-regional concerns are profoundly intermixed with those of their colleagues. Most of them have a single passion, taken very seriously—for one it is helping California salmon to spawn directly by hand, for another it is planting something like 20,000 trees, for a third it is cleaning up a polluted river, for another it is cataloguing all the edible wild plants of the mid-grass prairie (no, I'm not kidding, I know these people)— but they realize full well that these passions cannot be isolated, that the wisdom of bioregionalism is in its holism, its understanding of the connectedness of all things in the web of life.

· · ·

The bioregional movement in America generates even further resonance as a real possibility because it is unmistakably a part of what has become a worldwide movement of ecological politics, given various local names in various places but known now almost everywhere by the single sobriquet: Green.

Green politics, wherever it is found, is the introduction of ecological concerns into the political arena, where they are so badly needed and where they have been for so long missing, to our great and accumulating danger. It has now emerged in nearly every industrial country in the world,* and in several of them—most notably West Germany and Belgium—it has scored electoral successes with full-fledged Green parties. The West German movement in particular has attracted worldwide attention, not only for its dramatic tactics and skillful electoral strategies but also for the depth and boldness of its analysis. Its platform says, for example:

> Our policy is a policy of active partnership with nature and human beings. It is most successful in self-governing and self-sufficient economic and administrative units, of a humanly surveyable size. We stand for an economic system oriented to the necessities of human life today and for future generations,

*Australia, Austria, Belgium, Britain, Canada, Denmark, Finland, France, Ireland, Japan, Sweden, Switzerland, West Germany.

to the preservation of nature and a careful management of natural resources. We want a society which is democratic and in which relations between people and with nature are handled with increased awareness.

In this country Green politics is still nascent, but there are already local Green movements in California, Oregon, Tennessee, New York, Maine, New Hampshire, and Vermont, and in the last few years there have been several attempts to establish a nationwide network of Green-oriented organizers and groups. The Citizens Party has tried to develop a specifically Green perspective—at one point it was calling itself the American representative of the German Greens, though it had never quite endorsed any Green policies—and at least a half-dozen other groups, from the Movement for a New Society, a small Green Party in the Midwest, and even, *mirabile dictu*, the Yippies, have adopted Green ideas and terminology. The Bioregional Congress produced a Green caucus and, from that, a Green Organizing Committee with regional outposts across the country and an ongoing Green Committees of Correspondence to refine the message and develop grassroots support.*

It will be some time before the exact form of America's Green politics works itself out, but to be successful it will perforce be regionally grounded and it will have to understand itself in bioregional terms, as bioregionalism's political face. It will need to take the bioregional message into all the niches of the established system, whether that means appearing before a township planning commission, or running candidates for a county water board, or electing an ecologically oriented slate to a city council, or petitioning a regional air-pollution authority, or lobbying the state fish-and-game office, or influ-

*Later called The Greens/Green Party USA.

175

encing a state legislature's environment committee, or pressuring the staff of the Federal Environmental Protection Agency, or someday establishing a national party and electing a President committed to bioregional empowerment. American politics has always been complicated and protean because the country is so vast and diverse, but as long as it is clear in its bioregional vision, Green politics can be every bit as variegated—allotropic, let us say—and establish itself at least as a necessary alternative across the land.

. . .

Finally, there are two respects in which the bioregional vision can commend itself, less concrete than those enumerated above but not less important. For me they go to the soul of the bioregional concept, to show in simplest terms why its dreams of things that never were are not impractical wisps and vapors.

First, it has the virtue of *gradualism*. It suggests that the processes of change—first of organizing, educating, activating a constituency, and then of reimagining, reshaping, and recreating a continent—are slow, steady, continuous, and methodical, not revolutionary and cataclysmic. Inherent in the goal is the process, for like Gaea herself, the movement toward the bioregional future will have to be homeorrhetic or it will do irreparable violence to its own values—and in doing so will fail.

One cannot imagine bioregionalism being installed by revolution, no matter whose revolution it is, if for no other reason than that revolutions almost never produce the *contrariety* but the *continuation* of what they have replaced—and how, really, could they ever do else?—and a bioregional civilization would obviously have to be vastly different from the industrio-scientific one we now have. The trouble with revolutions, as Robert Frost once noted, is that by definition they go full circle and lead us back to where we came from. Bioregionalism would ideally be a *half*-revolution, a 180-degree turn, and that sort of change is so sweeping it could not possibly be imposed by a small cadre or dictated from without.

The bioregional project has to be an evolutionary one. It is only by a long and regular process of awakening, education, study, revision, faith, and experimentation that people will ease themselves into such a society. They must come to see that the various alternative futures they have been offered are senseless or downright dangerous, and they must appreciate that something like the bioregional future is the only sane choice for the survival of species other than the cockroach. And then they must learn what old ways have to be discarded and what new perceptions have to be honed, and learn how to give full rein to those cooperative and communal and participatory selves, those symbiotic and responsible and multi-dimensional selves, that had been blunted and confined before. That strikes me as a proceeding requiring some time, some patience.

Which is not the same as saying there is no urgency. The need for transformation is all too apparent, more so with every passing day. We do not know, and cannot, how long we have before the apocalypse, but it may be as imminent as the carbon-dioxide doomsters predict. This uncertainty can mean only that we should start the task of winning adherents immediately—begin the gradual process, since we know it has to be gradual, with all due speed and commitment.

In addition, the bioregional project has the virtue of *realism*. It does not demand any elaborate wrenching of the physical or human conditions of the world we know, any fantastic alterations of nature-as-it-is or people-as-they-are.

It does not posit, on the one hand, the violent technological interference with the world that so many scientistic visions of the future do. There is nothing here, for example, requiring that icebergs be floated from the polar seas to the equatorial deserts to provide drinking water; or proposing that the northern half of the Great Plains be given over to huge nuclear-power installations, protected by rings of fences and armaments, to provide electricity in an oil-depleted world; or creating enormous floating colonies in space to provide entirely controlled and human-managed environments when this one becomes uninhabitable.

And it does not presume, on the other hand, some new kind of superhuman being devoid of all the petty faults and errancies we know have characterized people in the past. A bioregional world does not ask, for example, for anything on the order of those ideologies that imagine, and promise to achieve, "a new socialist man," someone no longer interested in material goods or profits and incentives, no longer given to self-interest. Nor does it depend on the sort of conversion—a "transformation," as some are calling it—envisioned by those crusaders who say that, if only we educate the children in the right things, or if only we all understood the swami's teachings, or if only we all were conditioned by proper Freudian therapy, human error would be dispelled and the New World would come about.

On the contrary, the bioregional vision is much more—the expression seems fittingly Gaean—down to earth. No new technologies are necessary, nor any special techniques of making and doing beyond the ones we know now; on the technical side, the object is probably more to rediscover and relearn than to find new breakthroughs in robotics and circuitry. Nor, of course, are vast—and vastly complex and costly—projects necessary, since problems in general become smaller as the territory does, and working out ways to supply renewable energy for 1 million or 2 million or 10 million people is infinitely simpler than for 250 million.

Because it is basic to the bioregional ideal of diversity that we take people as they are and insist on letting them behave in their diverse ways in their own separate habitats, there is no need or desire to remold them all to some imaginative and impossible design. Bioregionalism does require a certain amount of shifting of attitudes and rethinking of premises, as I have noted, and a rough sort of common understanding of the bedrock Gaean truths; but nothing wrenching, really, nothing that has not been thought and felt before by all kinds of people, nothing more than the wisdom of our forebears and the experience of our predecessors. To come to know one's region, to understand its ecological imperatives, to appreciate certain basic Gaean principles is so simple and organic a process that it is available, one has to believe, to any person open to it. Once that is understood, there is any amount of other sorts of knowledge and lore—or even miseducation and misunderstanding—that can be added on, any tenet or religion or ideology, permitting again the diversity of thought requisite for a diverse planet.

. . .

The bioregional project, then, certainly has its full measure of dreams of things that never were; yet when properly understood in its totality, it is not in any sense fantastical, chimerical, quixotic, or illusory. I do not suggest that it is inevitable or fated, or that once begun it could not be frustrated and defeated; just that it is without doubt possible. It is so well-grounded in the past, so much a part of the living present, so congruent with a practical future, that one does not have to be a dreamer to appreciate its value and its potential.

Of course it does not hurt to ask, over and over again, that most elemental human question, *Why not?*—for, as the Biblical admonition has it, "Where there is no vision the people perish."

179

IV

The Bioregional Imperative

To know harmony means to be in accord with the eternal. To be in accord with the eternal means to be enlightened.

Lao Tzu, *Tao te Ching*

This small, blue-green planet is the only one with comfortable temperatures, good air and water, a wealth of animals and plants, for millions (or quadrillions) of miles: a little water-hole in the Vast Space, a nesting place, a place of singing and practice, a place of dreaming. . . . We are all natives here, and this is our only sacred spot.

Gary Snyder, "Wild, Sacred, Good Land"

TWELVE

Gaea Confirmed

SOMETIME in the late 1960s British scientist James Lovelock, an independent chemist then at work with a few colleagues on studies of the earth's atmosphere, evolved the theory that the various systems of the planet—the biosphere, the hydrosphere, the atmosphere, all that goes to make up the world as we know it—seemed to behave in such a unitary and interconnected fashion that they could in some sense be said to constitute a single living organism, actually, scientifically *alive*.

As he later reported it to the scientific world in the pages of *New Scientist*:

> It appeared to us that the Earth's biosphere is able to control at least the temperature of the Earth's surface and the composition of the atmosphere. Prima facie, the atmosphere looked like a contrivance put together cooperatively by the totality of living systems to carry out certain necessary control functions. This led to the formulation of the proposition that living matter, the air, the oceans, the land surface, were parts of a giant system which was able to control temperature, the composition of the air and sea, the pH of the soil and so on as to be optimal for survival of the biosphere. The system seemed to

exhibit the behaviour of a single organism, even a living creature.

It was a stunning idea and totally unprecedented in contemporary science, but it gradually accumulated such a body of supportive evidence that Lovelock felt it could be expressed as a formal hypothesis, and he went in search of an appropriate name for it. Fortunately Nobel prize–winning author William Golding was working in the same village, and when sought out and asked his suggestion he was, Lovelock reported, unhesitating: "He suggested Gaia—the name given by the ancient Greeks to their Earth goddess."

Thus was born what Lovelock persisted in misspelling as the "Gaian" hypothesis (it is from here that the confusion of pronunciation stems), a sophisticated, coherent, contemporary confirmation of the very perception that all those millennially ancient cultures had evolved and that the early Greeks had named and embodied in the Western world.

• • •

In the years since then Lovelock has gone on to elaborate his hypothesis in his small book *GAIA: A New Look at Life on Earth*, which appeared in 1979, and to win a number of other scientists to its decidedly unorthodox banner. It is still in a working stage and still to be completely confirmed, but from the body of evidence assembled so far, it rests on three fairly solid cornerstones.

1. *Temperature.* If the earth were really inanimate, Lovelock argues, it could not have regulated its surface temperature as regularly and efficiently as we know it has over the last 3.5 billion years or so since the beginning of life.

The earth gets its heat from the sun, obviously, but the heat has *increased* by at least 30 percent (some say 70 percent) in those 3.5 billion years because the sun, like any other growing star, has increased its output of radiation. But if the earth were 30 percent colder those eons ago, it would have been a dead and frozen sphere quite incapable of supporting life—even a 2 percent drop in radiation causes an ice age, and a 30 percent decrease would mean complete global freezing—and therefore there must have been some sort of regulating process at work. Similarly, the sun's increasing radiation over those billions of years would have heated the earth's surface until the oceans boiled and life became impossible, if there were no intervening mechanisms. But in fact throughout all that time, even with the constantly changing output from the sun, the average temperature of the earth since the beginning of life has stayed at an astonishingly constant level between 10 and 20 degrees centigrade.

Lovelock does not attempt to explain the exact biotic processes that achieve this amazing regulation in the present world, but he does suggest that the biospheric production of ammonia was responsible for regulating heat during the very earliest phases of life. Carl Sagan and others have theorized that ammonia, then far more abundant than today, helped to form a thermal blanket during that period when the sun's radiance was so much weaker, and this protection permitted life to flourish. If over the long epochs the biosphere had been clumsy or inexact in this task, if in fact it had not been absolutely precise, life would not have survived: if there had been any *less* ammonia in the atmosphere, surface heat would have escaped, temperatures would have fallen, the land would be covered by ice, the sun's rays would be increasingly reflected, and eventually the earth would be a frozen, empty, lifeless sphere like Mars; if on the other hand there had been any *more* ammonia, even by a little, solar heat would be increasingly trapped, temperatures would rise, water vapor and other gasses (such as carbon dioxide) would build up a greenhouse effect, temperatures of 100 degrees centigrade would destroy the biosphere, and eventually the earth would be a hot, soggy, lifeless planet like Venus.

The purposeful way the earth seems to have regulated its temperatures to avoid the fate of its two nearest neighbors, and the ways it has continued to do so over these billions of years, seem to indicate a complex mechanism similar to those that regulate temperature in a beehive or a human being. Seem to indicate, in fact, life creating the optimal conditions for itself.

2. *Atmosphere.* The composition of the earth's atmosphere during the last 3.5 billion years has remained virtually constant *and* in the precise proportions that are necessary to sustain life. This perfect balance of gasses is so phenomenal as to seem highly improbable without imagining some form of intricate and regular monitoring and adjusting processes in constant operation on the earth's surface.

For example, the exact balance of methane and oxygen in the atmosphere has remained roughly constant during most of life on earth, a precise relationship that assures just the right amount of oxygen for life's continuance. That special combination could happen only by adding at least a billion tons of new methane into the atmosphere every year and at least twice as much oxygen, and there is no other source to produce that amount of gas except the biological activity on the earth itself. The complexity and accuracy of mechanisms required to assure that production on such a scale certainly suggests some kind of deliberate, one is tempted to say even conscious, manipulation.

Or take oxygen itself, that most essential product of the biosphere. It is continually reacting with other gasses like nitrogen, methane, and hydrogen (each of which is unstable in the presence of the others), so it might be expected to be highly erratic and variable. Yet its concentration remains constant, and constant to a special exactness: if the atmosphere contained any more oxygen, even by 3 or 4 percent, it would be such a congenial nurturer of fire that with the first lightning bolt the earth would be enveloped in flames; and if it contained any less, plant and animal life would expire.

There is only one rational explanation in Lovelock's view for the atmosphere, a complex balance of at least a dozen essential elements, having been maintained for 3.5 billion years in just the right mix necessary to sustain life, despite gasses being lost or recombined continuously and radiation levels increasing in intensity by a third. The explanation is that the atmosphere performs a precise function and is controlled to continue that function.

This atmospheric mix is—there is no other phrase for it—highly improbable. It is possible to calculate what a theoretical steady-state world would look like in which all of the hundred-plus chemical elements of the earth were brought to a thermodynamic equilibrium by the known rates of chemical reactions. The earth is nothing like that at all. Lovelock shows that the amounts of methane, nitrous oxide, and even nitrogen in our atmosphere are so far from this theoretical mix as to constitute "a violation of the rules of chemistry to be measured in tens of order of magnitude." His conclusion:

> Disequilibria on this scale suggest that the atmosphere is not merely a biological product, but more probably a biological construction: not living, but like a cat's fur, a bird's feathers, or the paper of a wasp's nest, an extension of a living system designed to maintain a chosen environment.

3. *Hydrosphere.* The salt content of the earth's oceans is about 3.4 percent, which is not so surprising, but it has re-

mained constant at about that level for several billion years, which is.

Because of the salt runoff from the land and the sea-floor's own production of salt, the saline levels of the oceans should increase by about 10 percent every 240 million years—or, over the last 3.5 billion years, by about 2000 percent. The oceans would long ago have become immensely briny salt ponds, far too salty to sustain any marine life, too salty in fact to permit successful land life. But obviously that has not happened, and in fact there appear never to have been any great variations in salinity in all that time.

This extraordinary—and for human life vital—balance is so ordered that it is hard to believe it is accidental; some process must be at work regularly removing and burying salinity purposefully and skillfully to permit the continuance of life. Lovelock does not pretend to know exactly what it is, but he points to two well-recognized phenomena: first, that small marine organisms construct huge coral and stromatolitic reefs, perhaps with the aim of creating immense shallow lagoons, like the shallow ponds on the ocean fringes where salt evaporates most rapidly; and second, that tiny ocean organisms called diatoms absorb surface-level silicates and, when they die and sink, transport the silicates to the bottom of the ocean to be eventually buried. Either or both of these phenomena may be the biotic devices that control salinity, part of the cybernetic system that works so well it begins, inescapably, to seem purposeful.

. . .

To date these Gaean postulates form only a hypothesis and, in view of the way the scientific establishment inevitably resists such novel ideas, it may be some time before they are adequately tested and proven or disproven. So far, though, there have been at least two demonstrations of the validity of the hypothesis to lend it considerable credence.

The first was a search in the atmosphere for certain "carrier compounds" that Lovelock guessed must exist as the means by which vital life chemicals such as iodine and sulfur are conveyed out of the ocean, where they are abundant, to the land, where they are scarce and badly needed. Such compounds had never been found and were not known to exist, but Lovelock followed his hypothesis and went in search of them. He found them: methyl iodide and dimethyl sulfide, two compounds directly produced by marine life, were discovered in the atmosphere.

The second demonstration was Lovelock's creation of a mathematical model called a "Daisy World." His idea was to prove that organisms can and do respond to—and in turn *regulate*—temperatures for their optimum life, and his model used light and dark daisies reacting to sunlight. The model is complex, but it demonstrates that the dark daisies spread faster at low temperatures, the light ones at higher, and between the two they work toward maintaining a steady surface around an optimal 20 degrees centigrade; apparently, therefore, thermal control by the ordinary processes of the biosphere is perfectly plausible. "The radical insight delivered by Daisy World," reported two scientific investigators in *The Ecologist*, "is that global homeorrhesis is in principle possible without the introduction of any but well-known tenets of biology."

Even before all the confirmatory work is done, however, other, independent scientists have come to similar conclusions. Lynn Margulis, a researcher at Boston University, concluded from her own work testing Lovelock's:

[It] is highly unlikely that chance alone accounts for the fact that temperature, pH, and the concentration of nutrient ele-

ments have been for immense periods of time just those optimal for life. . . . It seems rather more likely that energy is
expended by the biota actively to maintain these conditions.

Two Japanese scholars reported in 1983 that, based on their
work examining the earth's hydrological systems:

We can say that the earth is "living" too. The ecocycle (or
biosphere in a more popular terminology) is a subsystem of
the "living earth."

And Dr. Lewis Thomas, who gives no indication that he knows
Lovelock's work, has nonetheless come to a similar conclusion
by his own means:

Except for us, the life of the planet conducts itself as though it
were an immense, coherent body of connected life, an intricate
system, even, as I see it, an organism. An embryo, maybe,
conceived, as each one of us when first brought to life, as a
single successful cell.

It is not too soon, I believe, for us to acknowledge at least
the highly probable existence of a biosphere working to adapt
its environment in a myriad ways to assure the conditions for
survival. That the air, the oceans, the temperatures, all the
systems of earth for unimaginable years have been operating
in just those ways that maintain the conditions optimal for life
has no other credible explanation.

Whether one then wants to say that the earth is in fact "living" probably depends on one's definition of *life*, and that is a
thorny thicket indeed.* But it seems beyond doubt that such

---

*The standard life-science definition, formulated by Erwin Schrödin-
ger in his celebrated *What Is Life?*, is that which attracts "a stream of
negative entropy to itself, to compensate the entropy increase it pro-
duces by living, and thus to maintain itself on a stationary and fairly

an existence could not prevail if it were not in some sense *purposeful*, the product of an organized and self-regulated process, the same as we would find with a colony of microbes, or an ant hill—or a human being. We need not imply overt consciousness or superarching intention—there is no point in being metaphysical or teleological about this—for us to be able to speak of life, or something very much like it, in the totality and intermeshing of the systems of the earth.

. . .

And so, after all, the Greeks seem to have been right. There is no real doubt about it: the earth, the biosphere, is alive, "a living creature, one and visible, containing within itself all living creatures."

What, finally, does that mean for humankind? What can, what should, that mean for those of us who now and in the probable future share its life? Let me once more invoke Lewis Thomas, not simply because he is a biologist of such renown but because he may safely be assumed to represent no particular ideology, to have no special political ax to grind. He says:

> Our deepest folly is the notion that we are in charge of the place, that we own it and can somehow run it. We are beginning to treat the earth as a sort of domesticated household pet, living in an environment invented by us, part kitchen garden, part park, part zoo. It is an idea we must rid ourselves of soon, for it is not so. It is the other way around. We are not separate beings. We are a living part of the earth's life, owned and op-

---

low entropy level." By that reckoning, the earth, which has continually absorbed and used "negative entropy" in the form of radiant heat from the sun, gravitational energy from the moon, and cosmic radiation from outer space to maintain a roughly stationary entropy level for these past 3.5 billion years, can be said to be alive.

erated by the earth, probably specialized for functions on its behalf that we have not yet glimpsed.

Which is nothing less than the simple message, the simple wisdom, of the bioregional vision.

It behooves us, as nothing in the long history of humankind so far has behooved us, to understand this wisdom and, before it is too late, to give up those unearthly, demonic practices that threaten in so many ways the fundamental forms of life—that threaten, it is not too much to argue, life itself. We must learn to make the idea of the goddess Gaea an intimate part of—no, I want to say, in some sense *the whole of*—our lives, so that there is no moment of our passage, no point in our decisions, when we are not conscious of her imperatives, her needs, her treasures.

That will not come about easily, I grant. But it *can* be done; it *must* be done. Even if it takes, as biologist John Todd has suggested, a change as profound and as sweeping as the one that accompanied the origination of agriculture some 10,000 years ago.

Because what other choice, really, do we have?

Bibliography and Notes

I. THE BIOREGIONAL HERITAGE

1. Gaea

Berman, Morris, *The Reenchantment of the World*, Cornell, 1981.

Frazer, James, *The Golden Bough*, abbreviated, Macmillan, 1951.

Graves, Robert, *The White Goddess*, Knopf, 1948.

Hughes, J. Donald, *The Ecologist* (Camelford, Cornwall, England), No. 2–3, 1983.

James, Edwin O., *The Ancient Gods*, Putnam's, 1960.

Spretnak, Charlene, ed., *The Politics of Women's Spirituality*, Anchor, 1982.

Stone, Merlin, *When God Was a Woman*, HBJ/Harvest, 1976.

P. 3, 4: Plato, Xenophon, in Hughes.

P. 4: "Hymn to Earth," from Thelma Sargent, *The Homeric Hymn*, Norton, 1973, my rendition.

P. 7: Forbes, *California Historical Quarterly*, September 1971.

P. 8–9: Lucius Apuleius, in Stone, p. 22, Robert Graves's rendition.

P. 10: Berman, p. 16.

P. 11: Thomas, *The Lives of a Cell*, Bantam, 1974, p. 170.

2. Gaea Abandoned

Myceneans

Hughes, J. Donald, *Ecology in Ancient Civilizations*, University of New Mexico, 1975.

Massey, Marshall, *Co-Evolution Quarterly*, Winter 1983.

Scully, Vincent, *The Earth, the Temple and the Gods*, Yale, 1979.

Trevor-Roper, H. R., *Men and Events*, Octagon (New York), 1957.

Science/Nature

Basalla, George, ed., *The Rise of Modern Science*, D.C. Heath, 1968.

Berman, op. cit.

Bookchin, Murray, *The Ecology of Freedom*, Cheshire (Palo Alto), 1982.

Ehrenfeld, David, *The Arrogance of Humanism*, Oxford, 1978.

Leiss, William, *The Domination of Nature*, Braziller, 1972.

Merchant, Carolyn, *The Death of Nature*, Harper & Row, 1980.

Mumford, Lewis, *The Myth of the Machine*, 2 vols., Harcourt, 1967, 1970.

Thomas, Keith, *Man and the Natural World: Changing Attitudes in England, 1500–1800*, Allen Lane (London), 1983, Pantheon, 1983.

Worster, Donald, *The Ecologist*, No. 5, 1983.

Science/Capitalism

Braudel, Fernand, *Civilization and Capitalism: 15th–18th Century*, Vols. 1–3, Harper & Row, 1982–84; *The Mediterranean and the Mediterranean World in the Age of Philip II*, Harper & Row, 1972.

Marsak, Leonard M., ed., *The Rise of Science in Relation to Society*, Macmillan, 1964.

Tawney, R. H., *Religion and the Rise of Capitalism*, Harcourt, 1926.

Wallerstein, Immanuel, *The Modern World-System*, Academic, 1975.
Whitehead, Alfred North, *Science and the Modern World*, Macmillan, 1925.
   P. 12: Trevor-Roper, p. 8.
   P. 13: Scully, p. 41.
   P. 16: Hooke, Newton, in Berman, pp. 47, 115.

3. The Crisis

Barnet, Richard, *The Lean Years*, Simon and Schuster, 1982.
Catton, William, *Overshoot*, Illinois, 1980.
Coates, Gary, ed., *Resettling America*, Brickhouse (Amherst), 1981.
Davis, W. Jackson, *The Seventh Year*, Norton, 1979.
Ehrenfeld, op. cit., and *Conserving Life on Earth*, Oxford, 1972.
Goldsmith, Edward, et al. (*The Ecologist*), *A Blueprint for Survival*, Penguin, 1972.
Gray, Elizabeth Dotson, *Green Paradise Lost*, Roundtable (Wellesley, MA), 1981.
Hamaker, John, *The Survival of Civilization*, Hamaker-Weaver (Potterville, MI), 1982.
MIT Study of Critical Environmental Problems, Caroll Wilson, ed., *Man's Impact on the Global Environment*, MIT Press, 1971.
Roszak, Theodore, *Where the Wasteland Ends*, Anchor, 1973.
Weisberg, Barry, *Beyond Repair*, Beacon, 1971.
Worldwatch Institute (Lester Brown et al.), *State of the World*, Norton, 1984.
   P. 27: Barnet, p. 37.
   P. 28: Ehrenfeld, *Conserving*, p. 329.
   P. 31: MIT, in Goldsmith, *Blueprint*, op. cit., p. 93.
      Ehrenfeld, *Conserving*, p. 353.
   P. 31–32: Coates, p. 21.
   P. 32–33: Catton, pp. 170–73; p. 232; 213.

P. 34–36: Hamaker, John, *Solar Age or Ice Age? Bulletins*, Nos. 1–5 (Burlingame, CA 94010), "Comments," October 1983, November 1983.

II. THE BIOREGIONAL PARADIGM

4. Dwellers in the Land

Berg, Peter, ed., *Reinhabiting a Separate Country*, Planet Drum (San Francisco), 1978.

Raise the Stakes, Planet Drum, Fall 1979–.

Schumacher, E. F., *Small Is Beautiful*, Harper Torchbooks, 1973.

Snyder, Gary, in *The Schumacher Lectures*, Vol. II, Blond & Briggs (London), 1984; and interview, *Mother Earth News*, September-October, 1984.

P. 41: AE, *The Interpreters*, Macmillan, 1922, p. 60.

P. 42: Berry, speech to the North American Bioregional Congress, May, 1984.

P. 46: Schumacher, *Good Works*, Harper, 1979, p. 140.

P. 47: Weil, *The Need for Roots*, Putnam's, 1952, p. 52.

P. 49n.: Thomas, *Lives of a Cell*, op. cit., p. 89.

5. Scale

Kohr, Leopold, *The Breakdown of Nations*, Dutton, 1978; *The City of Man*, Puerto Rico, 1976; *Development Without Aid*, Christopher Davies (Wales), 1973; *The Overdeveloped Nations: The Diseconomies of Scale*, Schocken, 1977.

Mumford, Lewis, *The City in History*, Harcourt, 1961; *The Condition of Man*, Harcourt, 1944; *The Culture of Cities*, Harcourt, 1938.

Sale, Kirkpatrick, *Human Scale*, Coward-McCann, 1980; Perigee (Putnam's), 1982.

Schumacher, *Small Is Beautiful*, op. cit.

van Dresser, Peter, *Development on a Human Scale*, Praeger, 1972.

Bioregional mapping

Baker, O. E., *Atlas of American Agriculture*, U.S. Department of Agriculture, U.S. Government Printing Office, 1918–36.

Beale, Calvin, in *Alternatives to Confrontation*, Victor Arnold, ed., D.C. Heath, 1980.

Birdsale, Stephen S., and John W. Florin, *Regional Landscapes of the United States and Canada*, Wiley, 1978.

Browne, Jason, *The Secular Ark: Studies in the History of Biogeography*, Yale, 1983.

Hart, F., *Regions of the United States*, Harper, 1972.

Hunt, Charles B., *Natural Regions of the United States and Canada*, W. H. Freeman, 1974.

Indian Land Claims and Treaty Areas of North America, map, C.I.M.R.A., 1981, from Northern Sun Alliance, 1519 E. Franklin, Minneapolis, MN 55404.

Kroeber, A. L., *Cultural and Natural Areas of Native North America*, California, 1939.

National Resources Committee, *Regional Factors in National Planning and Development*, U.S. Government, 1935.

Symons, L., *Agricultural Geography*, Praeger, 1967.

U.S. Geological Survey, *National Atlas of the U.S.A.*, U.S. Government Printing Office, 1972.

Vishes, Stephen Sargent, *Climatic Atlas of the United States*, Harvard, 1954.

P. 62: Forest statistics, Lee R. Dice, *Natural Communities*, Michigan, 1952, p. 7.

P. 65: City of 1 million, A. Wolman, *Scientific American*, September 1965.

P. 66: *Blueprint*, Goldsmith, op. cit., p. 53.

6. Economy

Steady-state

Bookchin, *Toward an Ecological Society*, Black Rose (Montreal), 1980.

Boulding, Kenneth, *The Meaning of the Twentieth Century*, Harper & Row, 1964.

Daly, Herman E., *Steady-State Economics*, W. H. Freeman, 1977; ed., *Economics, Ecology, Ethics: Essays Toward a Steady-State Economy*, W. H. Freeman, 1973, 1980.

Georgescu-Roegen, Nicholas, *The Entropy Law and the Economic Process*, Harvard, 1971.

Henderson, Hazel, *The Politics of the Solar Age*, Anchor, 1981.

Johnson, Warren, *Muddling Toward Frugality*, Sierra Club Books, 1978.

Joint Economic Committee, U.S. Congress, *The Steady State Economy*, Vol. 5 of *U.S. Prospects for Growth*, U.S. Government Printing Office, 1976.

Meadows, Dennis, ed., *Alternatives to Growth*, Ballinger (Cambridge), 1977.

Mishan, E. J., *The Costs of Economic Growth*, Praeger, 1969.

Ophuls, William, *Ecology and the Politics of Scarcity*, W. H. Freeman, 1978.

Sale, *Human Scale*, op. cit., pp. 329–342.

Valaskakis, Kimon, et al., *The Conserver Society*, Harper & Row, 1979; Vols. 1–4, Conserver Society Project (GAMMA, 3535 Queen Mary Rd., Montreal).

Cooperative economy

Clastres, Pierre, *Society Against the State*, Urizen (New York), 1977.

Dalton, George, *Tribal and Peasant Economies*, Natural History, 1967.

Harris, Marvin, *Cannibals and Kings*, Random House, 1977.

Love, J. R. B., *Stone Age Bushmen of Today*, Blackie & Sons (London), 1936.

Pfeiffer, John, *The Emergence of Man*, Harper & Row, 1972.

Polanyi, Karl, *The Great Transformation*, Beacon, 1957; *Primitive, Archaic and Modern Economics*, Beacon, 1971; *The Ecologist*, No. 1, 1974.

Sahlins, Marshall, *Stone Age Economics*, Aldine (Chicago), 1972.

Community Land Trusts

Coates, Gary, *Resettling America*, op. cit.

Community Land Association, *Handbook*, White Oak Community Center (Duff, TN 37729), 1982.

Institute for Community Economics, *The Community Land Trust Handbook*, Rodale, 1982.

Matthei, Chuck, in *Catholic Rural Life*, No. 7, 1981; *Sojourners Magazine*, November 1979; *Community Economics*, Institute for Community Economics, 1982.

Swann, Robert, *The Community Land Trust: A Guide to a New Model for Land Tenure in America*, Center for Community Economic Development, 1972.

Whyte, William F., ed., *Economic Democracy and Locally Based Development Strategies*, U.S. Department of Labor, 1982.

Local economies

Dahlberg, Arthur, *How to Save Free Enterprise*, Devin-Adair (Old Greenwich, CN), 1974; *Money in Motion*, John De Graff, 1962.

Gesell, Silvis, *The Natural Economic Order*, Free Economy Association (Huntington Park, CA), 1920.

Greco, Tom, *Just Economics*, Peace and Justice Education Center (Rochester, NY), 1984.

Gregg, Richard B., *The Big Idol*, Navajivan Publishing (Ahmedabad, India), 1963 (available from Community Service, Box 243, Yellow Springs, OH 45387).

Hayak, F. A., *Denationalisation of Money*, Institute of Economic Affairs (London), 1976.

Jacobs, Jane, *Cities and the Wealth of Nations*, Random House, 1984.

Loomis, Mildred, *Alternative Americas*, Universe (New York), 1982.

Morgan, Griscom, "The Community's Need for an Economy," Community Service, 1969.

Swann, Robert, "Bootstrap Community Revitalization" and "An Independent Currency for the Berkshires," E. F. Schumacher Society (Box 76, RD 3, Great Barrington, MA 01230), n.d.

Turnbull, Shann, *Self-Financing Techniques for Enterprise Development Projects; What Everyone Should Know About Banking and Money—Especially Bankers and Economists*, E. F. Schumacher Society, n.d.; and *Democratising the Wealth of Nations*, self-published.

Whitehead, Geoffrey, *The Story of Money*, Usborne (London), 1975.

P. 67–68: Goldsmith, *The Ecologist*, No. 4, 1984; see also *The Ecologist*, No. 4, 1977.

P. 70: Daly, *Economics*, op. cit., p. 6.

P. 76: Substitutability, Alvin Weinberg and H. E. Geoller, *Science*, February 4, 1976.

P. 80: Pliny Fisk, *Bioregions and Biotechnologies*, 1983, Center for Maximum Potential Building Systems (8604 FM 969, Austin TX 78724).

P. 81: Goldsmith, op. cit. (1977).

Margulis, *Symbiosis in Cell Evolution*, W. H. Freeman, 1981; and see Bookchin, *Ecology of Freedom*, op. cit.

P. 82–83: Schumacher, *Small Is Beautiful*, op. cit., pp. 41–42.

P. 86–88: John Friedmann and Clyde Weaver, *Territory and Function: The Evolution of Regional Planning*, California, 1979, pp. 200–201.

P. 88: Borgese, in Coates, op. cit., p. 78.

7. Polity

Barclay, Harold, *People Without Government*, Kahn & Averill/ Cienfuegos (London), 1982.

Bookchin, *The Ecology of Freedom*, op. cit.; *Toward an Ecological Society*, op. cit.

Clastres, *Society Against the State*, op. cit.

Darling, Fraser, and John P. Milton, eds., *Future Environments of North America*, Natural History Press, 1966.

Gutkind, E. A., *Community and Environment*, Philosophical Library (New York), 1954.

Isaacs, Harold R., *Idols of the Tribe*, Harper & Row, 1975.

Jolly, Allison, *The Evolution of Primate Behavior*, Macmillan, 1972.

Leacock, Eleanor Burke, *Myths of Male Dominance*, Monthly Review, 1981.

Lee, Dorothy, *Freedom and Culture*, Prentice-Hall, 1959.

Maas, Arthur, ed., *Area and Power: A Theory of Local Government*, Free Press, 1959.

Middleton, John, and David Tait, *Tribes Without Rulers*, Routledge & Kegan Paul, 1958.

Odum, Eugene, *Fundamentals of Ecology*, W. B. Saunders, 1971.

Sale, *Human Scale*, op. cit.

Turnbull, Colin, *The Forest People*, Doubleday, 1962.

> P. 89: On Taoism, see Brian Morris, *Freedom*, August 21, 1981.
>
> P. 93–94: Isaacs, op. cit., pp. 5, 11.
>
> P. 97: Footnote: *Census of Governments*, U.S. Census Bureau, 1982.
>
> P. 99: Bookchin, *Ecology of Freedom*, op. cit., p. 29.
>
> P. 100–01: Clastres, op. cit., pp. 174, 178 ff.

8. Society

Coates, Gary, *Resettling America*, op. cit.

Goldsmith, Edward, *A Blueprint for Survival*, op. cit.

Schumacher, *Small Is Beautiful* and *Good Work*, op. cit.

Trager, William, *Symbiosis*, Van Nostrand, 1970.

Warfare

Bookchin, Murray, *Ecology of Freedom*, op. cit.

Bruyn, Severyn, and Paula Raymon, eds., *Creative Conflict in Society*, Wiley, 1978.

Carthy, John, ed., *The Natural History of Aggression*, Academic, 1964.

Diamond, Stanley, *In Search of the Primitive*, Transaction, 1981.

Durbin, E., and G. Catlin, eds., *War and Aggression*, Routledge & Kegan Paul (London), 1938.

Goldsmith, Edward, *The Ecologist*, No. 4, 1974; No. 2–3, 1983.

Horkheimer, Max, and Theodor Adorno, *Dialectic of Enlightenment*, Seabury (Continuum), 1972; Horkheimer, *The Eclipse of Reason*, op. cit.

Kohr, Leopold, *The Breakdown of Nations*, op. cit., Ch. 2.

McPhee, John, *La Place de la Concorde Suisse*, Farrar, Straus & Giroux, 1984.

Mead, Margaret, *Cooperation and Competition Among Primitive Peoples*, Beacon, 1961.

Mumford, Lewis, *The City in History*, op. cit.

Sharp, Gene, *Social Power and Political Freedom*, Beacon, 1980; *The Politics of Nonviolent Action*, Porter Sargent, 1974.

P. 111: Thomas, *New York Times*, June 7, 1983, p. C1.

P. 113: Trager, op. cit., p. vii.

P. 114: Schumacher, *Good Work*, op. cit., pp. 46–7.
    Jacobs, *Cities*, op. cit.

P. 124: Schmookler, Andrew, *The Parable of the Tribes*, California, 1984, p. 21.

P. 128: Kohr, op. cit., p. 91.

P. 129: Rathje and settlement sizes, Sale, *Human Scale*, op. cit., pp. 179 ff., 455 ff., 482 ff.

P. 130: Jacobs, op. cit., pp. 214–15.

III. THE BIOREGIONAL PROJECT

9. Past Realities

Turner

F. J. Turner, *The Significance of Sections in American History*, Holt, 1932, reprint 1950; *The United States, 1830–50*, Holt, 1935, reprint 1958; *American Sociological Society Papers*, Vol. II, 1908; and see James D. Bennett, *Frederick Jackson Turner*, Twayne, 1975.

Mumford

in Carl Sussman, ed., *Planning the Fourth Migration: The Neglected Vision of the Regional Planning Association of America*, MIT, 1976, reprinting the *Survey Graphic*, May 1925; *The Culture of Cities*, Harcourt, 1938; see also, *Technics and Civilization*, Harcourt, 1934, esp. Ch. VI.

Odum

Odum and Harry Estill Moore, *American Regionalism*, Holt Rinehart, 1938, reprint 1966; Odum and Katharine Jacker, eds., *In Search of the Regional Balance of America*, North Carolina, 1945; Odum, *Southern Regions of the United States*, North Carolina, 1936; see also Michael O'Brien, *The Idea of the American South, 1920–41*, Johns Hopkins, 1979.

NRC

National Resources Committee, *Regional Factors in National Planning and Development*, December 2, 1935, U.S. Government Printing Office, containing the *Report of the Technical Committee on Regional Planning*, October 1935.

Jensen, Merrill, ed., *Regionalism in America*, Wisconsin, 1951.

McHarg, Ian, *Design With Nature*, Doubleday/Natural History, 1969.

P. 138–39: Turner, *Significance*, op. cit., pp. 47, 49, 38, 40.

P. 141–43: Mumford, in Sussman, op. cit., pp. 90, 92, 93.

P. 143–44: Mumford, *Culture*, op. cit., p. 386.

P. 144–46: Odum, *Regionalism*, pp. 277, 10–11.

P. 146–48: NRC, pp. 155, 144, 8, 23, 24, 179.

10. Present Currents

Separatism

Albery, Nicholas, and Mark Kinzley, *How to Save the World*, Turnstone (Wellingborough, Northhamptonshire, UK), 1984.

Co-Evolution Quarterly, Winter 1982.

Cummings, Richard, *Proposition Fourteen*, Grove, 1980.

Hobsbawm, Eric, *New Left Review*, September 1977.

Jacobs, Jane, *The Question of Separatism*, Random House, 1980.

Kohr, *The Breakdown of Nations*, op. cit.

Raise the Stakes, Planet Drum, 1979–.

Snyder, Louis L., *Global Mini-Nationalisms*, Glenwood (West-port, CN), 1982.

Zwerin, Michael, *A Case for the Balkanization of Practically Everyone*, Wildwood House (London), 1976; *Devolutionary Notes*, Planet Drum, 1980.

Regionalism

Alden, Jeremy, and Robert Morgan, *Regional Planning*, Wiley, 1974.

American Institute of Planners, *Planning America*, 1974.

Clavel, Pierre, ed., *Urban and Regional Planning in an Age of Austerity*, Pergamon, 1980.

Cumberland, John H., *Regional Development Experiences and Prospects in the United States*, Mouton (Paris), 1971.

Dickinson, *Regional Concept*, Routledge & Kegan Paul, 1976; *City and Region*, Routledge & Kegan Paul, 1964; *Regional Ecology*, Wiley, 1970.

Editorial Research Reports, *Resurgence of Regionalism*, February 1977.

Elliott, William Yandell, *The Need for Constitutional Reform*, Whittlesey House (New York), 1935, esp. pp. 191 ff.

Friedmann, John, and William Alonso, *Regional Policy*, MIT, 1975.

Friedmann, John, and Clyde Weaver, *Territory and Function*, op. cit.

Glikson, Artur, *The Ecological Basis of Planning*, Martinus Nijhoff (The Hague), 1971, edited by Lewis Mumford.

Hall, Peter, ed., *Europe 2000*, Columbia, 1977.

Hoover, Edgar M., *Introduction to Regional Economics*, Knopf, 1975.

Jackson, Gregory, et al. (Harvard-MIT Joint Center for Urban

Studies), *Regional Diversity*, Auburn House (Boston), 1981.

Lynch, Kevin, *Managing the Sense of a Region*, MIT, 1976.

Miernyk, William H., *Regional Analysis and Regional Policy*, Oelgeschlager, Gunn & Hein (Cambridge, MA), 1982.

Mumford, Lewis, *Regional Planning in the Pacific Northwest*, Northwest Regional Council, Portland, 1939.

Price, Kent A., *Regional Conflict and National Policy*, Johns Hopkins, 1982.

Sharkansky, Ira, *Regionalism in American Politics*, Bobbs-Merrill, 1970.

Smith, Carol A., ed., *Regional Analysis*, Academic, 1976, 2 vols.

    P. 152: On disintegration, *Human Scale*, op. cit., pp. 20–22; 430–33.

    P. 153: Isaacs, op. cit., p. 4.

    P. 154: Hobsbawm, op. cit.

        Snyder, op. cit.

    P. 156: Zwerin, op. cit., p. 4.

    P. 157: Clout, Hugh, ed., *Regional Development in Western Europe*, John Wiley, 1981, p. 15.

        Shahabuddin, in *The Guardian*, July 18, 1983, p. 11.

    P. 158: Thurow, *The Zero-Sum Society*, Basic, 1980.

    P. 159: Harvard-MIT, in Jackson, op. cit., p. 5.

        Markusen, in Clavel, op. cit.

    P. 162: Special district governments, *U.S. Census of Governments*, U.S. Government Printing Office, 1982.

11. Future Visions

Bioregional library

Berg, Peter, ed., *Reinhabiting a Separate Country*, op. cit.

Berg, Peter, and George Tukel, *Bioregions: A New Context for Public Policy*, Planet Drum, 1980.

Bookchin, op. cit.

Dasmann, Raymond, *The Last Horizon*, Macmillan, 1963; *Planet in Peril*, UNESCO, 1972; *Ecological Principles for Economic Development*, Wiley, 1973.

Helm, Michael, *City Miner*, City Miner Books (San Francisco), 1983.

Mander, Jerry, *Four Arguments for the Elimination of Television*, Morrow, 1978.

Nabhan, Gary, *The Desert Smells Like Rain*, North Point (San Francisco), 1982.

Snyder, Gary, *Earth House Hold*, New Directions, 1969; *Turtle Island*, New Directions, 1974; *Songs for Gaia* [sic], Copper Canyon Press (Port Townsend, WA), 1979; *Axe Handles*, North Point (San Francisco), 1984.

Todd, John, and Nancy Jack Todd, *Bioshelters, Ocean Arks, City Farming*, Sierra Club, 1984.

Todd, John, and George Tukel, *Reinhabiting Cities and Towns: Designing for Sustainability*, Planet Drum, 1981.

Tukel, George, *Toward a Bioregional Model*, Planet Drum, 1982.

Worster, Donald, *Nature's Economy*, Sierra Club Books, 1977; Anchor, 1979.

P. 165: Lynch, op. cit., p. 10.

P. 172–73: Bioregional Congress, *North American Bioregional Congress Proceedings*, New Life Farm (Drury, MO), 1984.

P. 174–75: *Programme of the German Green Party*, Heretic Books (London), 1983, p. 7.

IV. THE BIOREGIONAL IMPERATIVE

12. Gaea Confirmed

Bookchin, Murray, *The Ecology of Freedom*, op. cit.

Co-Evolution Quarterly, Spring 1981, Fall 1984.

Hughes, J. Donald, *The Ecologist*, No. 2–3, 1983.

Lovelock, James, *GAIA* [sic], Oxford, 1979.

Margulis, Lynn, and Dorion Sagan, *The Ecologist*, No. 5, 1983.

Margulis, Lynn, *Symbiosis in Cell Evolution*, op. cit.

Tsuchida, Atsushi, and Takeshi Murota, *Social Science Review* (Sri Lanka), February 1983.
    P. 183–84: *New Scientist*, No. 65, 1975, p. 304.
    P. 187: Lovelock, op. cit., p. 10.
    P. 189–90: Margulis, op. cit., pp. 348ff.
            Japanese, Tsuchida and Murata, op. cit.
    P. 190–92: Thomas, *New York Times Magazine*, April 1, 1984.

Index